POWER PRESENTER!

The Fast track to World Class Presenting

Chris Cummins

& Glen McCoy

ISBN 978-0-9931739-0-5

ISBN 978-0-9931739-0-5

Contents

Dedicated to Speakers with Passion
and Presenters with Ambition
all over the world...

Foreword

Twenty years ago, the idea of standing up and presenting in front of a group of people was something that was never automatically expected of you. Yes there were always people prepared to do it and a few even volunteered, however if you were adamant that it wasn't your kind of thing, your inability, lack of interest or even fear was understood immediately. Today it's very different. In business and indeed a number of non business situations, the very idea of standing in front of a gathering of faces and staring back like a rabbit in the headlights is likely to be frowned upon, and those unaccustomed to making public speeches would stand a distinct disadvantage if they wanted to get ahead in their career or business.

Welcome to the world of *POWER PRESENTER!*

Since 2012, *Power Presenter!* has been a popular choice as a way of getting people on their feet and immediately feel confident to speak up. As creators of the programme, which has been lovingly crafted with psychology at its heart, we are proud of the roller coaster ride that nearly every participant has enjoyed and engaged with. But this book isn't meant to be marketing blurb, but a comprehensive manual that's almost as good as going on the one or two day extravaganza for yourself. You may consider this book as an alternative to going on a power presenter workshop, but it's important to be reminded that a skill like being an extraordinary communicator does depend on good live coaching with subsequent practice to test what you've learned, making sure it really works.

There are of course a myriad of courses, workshops and other good books out there on presentation skills and you may be forgiven for wondering what actually makes this contribution any different. It's a question we get asked often and one we take seriously as it would be too easy to gloss over it with a glib comment. The answer lays in the backstory.

Power Presenter! was originally conceived through two factors. One frustration and the second innovation. As a business, OTD was being asked to provide presentation skills training not just in the UK but on practically every continent and we used to deliver a selection of great tools and ideas, as one would expect in such a workshop. However it dawned on us that the subject itself differed from say 'selling effectively' or 'negotiation skills'. The stark reality was that giving presentations was not based on any formula. There was no known presenting model that people were using and therefore on public speaking courses, attendees would simply come away with a selection of useful ideas. Worse still, many courses were poorly put together and some didn't even encourage attendees to practise the techniques being shared. There's no question that presenting is in the same category as ski-diving, swimming, archery and tree surgery. It's highly practical and the theory behind it is as important was the act of doing it right from the start.

As an analogy, today, more medical schools get students 'practising' on patients from day one of their training, yet over thirty years ago most schools only introduced patients in year three. The other factor is having a model. If you are about to ski-dive on your own by the use of a static line, there is a model you are taught and expected to follow as you exit the aircraft for the first time.

It's a drill that you learn, and yes, one that's that's drilled into you as your life may depend on it. Presenting needs to have similar considerations and we are all aware that through lack of training, many would-be presenters 'die' on stage before they even complete their opening remarks.

So assuming there was a presenting model that you could learn and replicate with relative ease, what else might you need to learn? We suggest that the key ingredients to becoming a power presenter includes:

- a presenting model that works for anyone
- an easy way to create self-confidence
- a simple toolkit to back up the model
- the chance to practise with a coach one to one
- a methodology that can be implemented almost immediately
- a recipe to remove negative feelings and fears that are barriers to success

It's also about being able to get your audience to **lean forward** in your direction. You will read this phrase many times to remind you that the key goal of any power presenter is to capture attention both in mind and *physiology*.

Getting the Most from this Book

The chances are that you have already attended a *Power Presenter!* programme and want to use this book as an aide memoir to dip into from time to time, which is a good strategy.

In fact we have a chapter dedicated to graduates from *Power Presenter!* and ask you check out: "Presenting Gold", particularly before a major presentation where your skills may be measured against specific results and important outcomes. However if you are reading this book without any prior knowledge or experience of this programme, then we welcome you with open arms and hope that the contents will excite you sufficiently to take the plunge and book up for a workshop by contacting us through the OTD website: *www.otd.uk.com.*

For ease of approach, we have written this as if you the reader is in the latter category; someone new to the *Power Presenter!* approach. Like most books, start at Chapter 1 and work your way through making copious notes. If you are a mind mapper so much the better, and always remember that the best way to learn something is to teach someone else.

If you head up a team who need to be able to present, albeit internally within the business, then offer them tips chapter by chapter. Sessions need not be long, and you may be surprised how better presentation skills will go on to develop the individual in ways that you never thought possible.

Time and time again we have seen amazing transformations. In our one day version of the workshop participants are thrown into the deep end at the very beginning and asked to stand up and present for 2-3 minutes. Then at the end of the day, once more we ask the individuals to do the same thing, but now incorporating the tools they've learned. Those that use their new toolkit, normally make a positive and often major improvement to their presentation style, which also boosts their overall confidence at the same time.

It's interesting to note how many people link their confidence with their perceived ability to present to others; something they have carried around in their head since that first scary session in front of the class where the teacher being less than helpful, forced them to read in front of everyone without warning.

Often this single incident is the start of the so called fear of public speaking, and like any irrational fear that's been planted into someone's mind, it festers and grows over time. No wonder on many phobia polls, it comes out at number 1, where the fear of death is in say 8th position! The joke often shared about this, is that most people delivering the eulogy at a funeral would much rather be in the coffin!

A Presenting Model that Works for Anyone

How is it that over the decades the idea of a Presenting Model has been completely ignored and often considered as unnecessary or impractical? We raise our hands and say that we too were in this mindset once and the danger in not offering a model is that individuals who consider themselves as poor speakers then put their lack of success down to silly factors like their looks, low confidence, height, sex, scanty knowledge of their mother tongue, sense of humour or plain old lack of charisma. Without reservation, we can confirm that this list of factors can be set aside immediately because with the right model none of these reasons can hold up as valid.

The *Alphabet Presenting Model* is based on logic, common sense and human psychology. When baking a cake there are certain rules you need to apply in a set order of steps that is known to work every single time.

The model is called a recipe. Change the order or leave out key ingredients and you no longer get a delicious cake but a right royal mess that no one wants to eat. It's also not about experience. Children make great presenters with little or zero training. They also make delicious cakes by simply following the recipe. We devised and named the *Alphabet Presenting Model* for two reasons. The first was a way of being able to remember what the model is, and secondly as a structured way to dip into powerful tools as required. The A-F section covers the all important presenting model itself, while G-Z is a further 20 power tools that you can review and consider using in any presentation. So A-F is the completely necessary and G-Z is entirely optional.

An Easy Way to Create Self-Confidence

We don't keep it a secret that the two of us are Master NLP Practitioners and trainers qualified to use and teach the subject, as well as run courses and certify successful candidates. So NLP, or Neuro-Linguistic Programming, is layered within the programme, although for most people they would be unaware of the fact. Whatever your existing level of understanding or skill in the subject, we have incorporated the best and most appropriate NLP tools, which is one of the reasons *Power Presenter!* delivers such a hefty punch. And also using NLP, we help nervous presenters, and even those who believe they have a phobia about public speaking, to delete these feelings permanently. Then we help them to get going with a set of steps that anyone of any experience level can use almost immediately. It's also worth noting that 20% of all who attend our programmes are already great speakers.

Yet even these people, sometimes highly polished professionals, also get a great deal from the programme as a refresher or new insight into presenting concepts they have never considered before.

A Simple Toolkit to Back-Up the Model

The toolkit of 20 tools doesn't have to be used necessarily in every presentation. Yet most power presenters invariably want to try out new and exciting ways to stimulate and truly engage audiences. Many have reported back feeling on cloud nine when they are one of a group of keynote speakers and using power presentation 'technology' has made them stand head and shoulders above the rest. Certainly at the time of writing this edition of *Power Presenter!* we are confident that there are few tools we have overlooked, and we are certain that you need not look beyond the G-Z selection for all your skill requirements. Indeed, if you were to use as few as 2-3 tools in conjunction with the A-F model, your presentation is likely to be well delivered, very professional, and highly successful.

About the Authors

Chris Cummins started working as a Pharmaceutical Sales Representative in 1988 and realised very quickly that he had to do effective presentations on a daily basis to General Practitioners and Hospital doctors.

"The more I achieved promotions in my industry, the more I understood the importance of the way presentations needed to be put together to excite and enthuse 'the audience' to change their behaviour. At this point I met with Glen McCoy who has been one of the biggest catalysts to help me to change my perceptions on presenting.

He helped me to discover that the more we focus on our audience rather than ourselves, the more engaging we automatically become."

Chris is also co-founder of the Business Coaching company OTD UK Ltd and has coached presentation skills over the past decade to presenters from all sorts of cultures, backgrounds and capabilities all over the world.

Glen McCoy first started presenting at school and enjoyed it so much that he created a 'Lecture Circuit Group' of like minded individuals who had a passion for engaging audiences.

"Probably the first mistake I made was to ignore the need for tools and techniques. Whereas I got people's attention to start with, I also soon lost it quickly with my inexperience. However in 1986, I was about to write a book on successful entrepreneurs that ended up as a two-part presentation instead. This time I did some research on good presentation tools and this one event was probably the springboard to many future successful presentations. Having delivered many public speaking workshops for companies between 1997-2009, I soon found a kindred spirit in Chris Cummins who shared my desire to make public speaking a thing of the past and Power Presenting as a new methodology for the future."

Glen is also the author of many business books like 'Guerrilla Coaching' and has created coaching content for some of the world's largest brands.

Over to You

Now it's your turn. Here's wishing you every success in maximising the potency your future presentations as a fully trained *Power Presenter!*

Chris Cummins & Glen McCoy, 2015

Chapter 1

The Presenting Myth

Suddenly it grips you.

It starts with the awareness of discomfort. Hard to describe exactly what that sensation is, as it can be a different set of stimuli for different people. It's been colourfully described by some as 'the ground started to open up from under me' and 'I could feel that I was about to be swallowed whole' and 'I suddenly appeared to lose all control of basic functions; sudden word-loss, the ability to utter coherent sounds, make sense of what I was doing and above all courage'.

Gradually this uneasy feeling may manifest itself as a racing heartbeat, a sweaty brow and even a feeling of slight nausea. In extreme cases the individual is looking for an escape route from what seems to be worse than physical torture and death itself. These appear to be just some of the symptoms that occur when a person is asked to simply stand up and speak to a group of people in front of them.

Of course the fear that's associated with public speaking or what we prefer to call *presenting* is totally illogical. The same people who are challenged by presenting to an audience formally are normally very happy to present to one person or chat away in front of a group of their friends.

The mental barrier is about communicating with strangers. It's also interesting to note that there's a sliding scale at work.

At one end are people who are slightly uneasy but happy to carry on, while at the other end are those who are absolutely white-knuckle-weak-bladder-terrified. If this part of the scale measured 10 and the other less challenged end was 0, then most of the people who come to *Power Presenter!* workshops are between 1 and 7. We'd certainly like to encourage more in the 8-10 category but our challenge is getting them to attend since they assume there's nothing more they need to learn. The good news is we have a formula here within the pages of this book that may be used to improve anyone, regardless of where they are on the scale. Sometimes those polished presenters who do come along go away with smiles of satisfaction having gleaned one or two things that will make now a massive difference to their presenting.

Where Fear Originates

For many people, unbeknown to them, foundations of their fear come directly from childhood experiences.

- Fear through Ridicule

- Fear of a teacher

- Lack of positive feedback

- Peer pressure

- Jealous classmates undermining them

- Acceptance of other invalid myths

- The spider phobia phenomenon

Growing up can be a confusing, painful and disorientating business. If there is a lack of connection between a child and parents/siblings/teachers/friends, then the child finds themselves isolated, and the lack of confidence can manifest in all sorts of ways. In the past there have been far more children who stammered in class in comparison with the number that do so today. This has a lot to do with the change in connection between parents and children and teachers and children. Thankfully here in the UK, the 'stiff upper lip brigade' is a dying breed that destroyed the confidence of millions whilst thinking they were upholding traditional character building values. This had also seeped into traditionalist teachers of the past who believed that children should be seen and not heard encouraging old fashioned ridicule of a child in front of their classmates.

Another aspect is lack of positive feedback or basic encouragement from parents to their children. In some cultures it's deemed showing off to present in front of a group. Child peer pressure often motivated by jealousy has been anti-individual and pro the group as a whole.

From this basic understanding spawns the mass acceptance of other mythical ideas, such as volunteering is bad. Eventually the myth is accepted as a truth, and even today if you stand up in front of a group of 500 people and ask for a volunteer from the stage, however innocuous the request for help, you will get less than 1% putting their hands up, and occasionally no one at all.

The Spider Phobia Phenomenon

Take people who have a fear of spiders. With the right psychology, almost all of them would be able to dramatically lose the fear they have in a very short space of time. Many will also be able to completely extinguish the fear forever if they were shown how, and this applies to just about any irrational fear including public speaking.

Most spider phobics readily admit they have picked up this fear from their parents, who have brainwashed their children into accepting and adopting the very same fears that they were passed. Young children will observe the fear on the face of a parent escaping the demon spider without reference to the spider itself. It's not the spider that created the fear initially, it was the expression of fear on the face of the parent that created this new fear within them. Prior to the incident, the child had no view on spiders and certainly no fear. In certain parts of the world, instilling a fear of snakes in young children can be life-saving. If they didn't have any fear they would be tempted to pick up reptiles that can kill in a single bite.

However presenting in front of a group is unlikely to be life-threatening, and as parents we need to be aware of our responsibility to our off spring to help them to accept that presenting is an easy to do thing that can be fun, exciting and very satisfying. But what of those who understand this and still have the phobia gripping them metaphorically around the throat? Is there a quick cure?

The Big Red Balloon

The Big Red Balloon is a technique you could consider using. Imagine you have climbed into a hot air balloon on a beautifully sunny day. It's going to take you up into a mountain area where there's the most amazing view in a superb mountain top restaurant. Here people will be waiting to have lunch with you after listening to a presentation you have prepared.

You are very happy and can't wait to get there. However, as you climb in the basket and the balloon starts to lift, you imagine your twin self standing below with a frown. This person represents everything you fear in public speaking. Now as the balloon really takes off up towards the mountain restaurant you see the positive expressions of the people waiting to be your audience. Below is the face of your twin who's expression is entirely negative full of fear, but as the balloon sweeps you up, the face of your twin is getting smaller and smaller, and consequently you feel happier and happier until your twin's face disappears as you finally spot a sea of positive welcoming faces to greet you to speak. You feel great because you've managed to ditch your twin's negativity about the fear of presenting.

Do this technique once a day for 30 days and you will notice how your association with presenting changes. You genuinely feel different about it and in fact quite relish the idea. To any phobic this sounds mad and impossible, yet it wouldn't hurt to give it a whirl. Even better is the knowledge that you don't have to believe in this for it still to work. It's like exercise. Whether you believe in exercise or not, if you do it, it will make you look and feel healthier.

The Hara Technique

This alternative tool originates from martial arts and in particular, Kendo. Some people call Hara your personal power centre and it physiologically exists three inches above your navel in your lower abdomen.

1. Take a moment to locate it. Place three fingers above your navel. Just above your top finger is the Hara Position.
2. Now imagine your so called fear of presenting. Give it a score out of 10. Ten is terrified of speaking, and 0 is where you couldn't care less.
3. Stand up, keep your fingers on your abdomen if you wish, or place your hands by your side.
4. Now imagine you are in front of a large audience and notice your score out of 10.
5. Then focus your attention on the Hara Position as you look at your audience. In fact you've now changed the point of mental focus. You are focusing on a part of your physiology not the fear... and notice how this feels different.
6. Whether you sense this change or not, try it out several times. You could do it in any situation where you feel a lack of confidence. Even something like making a complaint about something in a shop or restaurant. Focus on the Hara Position first and notice how more in control you feel. Do this a few times and once you get the hang of it, apply it to the so called negative feeling about presenting, and notice how it starts to fade and eventually evaporate.

The Myth Explored

Then there's the so called myth around presenting. That it's only for the gifted and talented. Extroverts with supernatural abilities they were born with; super genes that have been passed down to them. People cite the fact that famous actors will have parents who were Hollywood stars and have children who will become similar success stories.

The myth is further developed by the long discussions around nurture versus nature and that not all of us were born to speak to groups of our fellow human beings. Actually the complete reverse is not only true, but makes much more logical and rational sense.

The fact is that you don't need any special abilities, gifts or talents to create awesome presentations. As already eluded to, take any group of children, the younger the better. How many of them would turn down an opportunity of standing up and doing a star turn of some sort with an audience? We have all done it and been there when very young. Yet as we grow older, suddenly from nowhere many of us become shrinking violets in any 'on stage or bright lights' situation. But times are changing and particularly in businesses all over the world, individuals are now expected to present their ideas, thoughts, dreams and aspirations very publicly to their colleagues and managers. Social media sites such as *YouTube* underpin this philosophy and our children may even obliterate the myth completely in our brave new communication rich world. However in the mean time, all of us need to shape up to the challenge of defeating the monster myth not only in ourselves but others around us.

The good news is that if you potentially have a quirky style, are hampered by a speech impediment or are unable to utter a single word for medical reasons, like Stephen Hawking, these factors will simply make you extra special in the eyes of an audience and therefore more likely to be a much bigger success ironicaslly. Nick Vujicic is a great example of an extraordinary power presenter. He's a guy larger than life. 'How tall is he?' you may be wondering. Well he was born without legs.

Then does he use amazing gestures when speaking? Actually he was also born without arms too. How good then is a limbless individual when presenting? Well you need to see him present.

He's awesome, jaw dropping and unquestionably world class. Check him out on *youtube* and discover all his other talents and attributes that put doubting Thomas presenters to shame. Fear is also totally subjective. One person's fear is another person's adrenaline rush. But with the right mindset, approach, and set of easy to use tools, everyone has the chance to realise the inner ability that they already own; to become a world class presenter in a very short timeframe indeed. The bottom line is that there are no excuses for being a poor presenter, particularly if you have been given a model with simple steps. By the end of reading this book, you'll definitely have acquired this.

What follows in this compact set of notes is a journey that's been designed for ease of understanding. The only requirement from your side is the desire to take the first step. The rest will fall into place allowing you to discover who you truly are in front of any audience, any size, anywhere in the world.

Now for the good news about the first step. You've actually already taken it! You're doing it now. Reading about presenting and therefore wanting to know more with hopefully an open mind. Are you ready for Step 2?

Chapter 2

The World's First Presentation Skills Model

The World's First Presenting model?   How so? Let's look this concept by first asking you to choose the odd one out below. Which one do you think it is?

- Movie
- Play
- Presentation
- Novel
- Song

There are many reasons why any of these could be the odd one out. For example, you could say that a movie is the only one where you can see the actors and locations in real settings as, whereas with all the others imagination is required.

You could say a play was the odd one out for the fact that it's possible to somehow get the audience involved, although the same can be said of a song when you're at a concert. You could be forgiven for thinking it's a song because when recorded you can play it over and over again as well as rewind it whenever you like, although the same can of course be said of a movie DVD.

So surely it must be a novel then, because it's the only one where the words and phrases the author has spent time crafting can be open to personal interpretation by the reader, but then you may say the same can be said of a movie or play.

The answer is much simpler, and as authors and presenters it's been staring at us in the face for years. Both of us have been on about half a dozen presentation skills workshops a piece over the past 20 years. All of the programmes taught us roughly the same thing... that presentation skills are a collection of established techniques around body language and voice. As for structure or a model it's *a good beginning, excellent middle and great ending* kind of thing. That's all very well, but how do you do this exactly? What's the formula for this? What is the model that anyone, regardless of their talent, can follow? Something so good in fact that a few simple steps later they will have been able to create an outstanding and highly professional presentation; one they can then dynamically deliver with success as a given?

So the answer to the odd one out question is **the presentation**. Before *Power Presenter!* no presentation skills workshop ever offered a model for public speaking. Finally there is one that we proudly call '*The Alphabet Presenting Model*' and the good news is that it's simple to learn, easy to master and creates awesome presentations time after time.

Now here's the spooky part.

]After coming up with this model, coaching it to groups all over the world and getting fantastic feedback, we then started to look at some of the most famous presentations ever on the net - particularly on YouTube - and suddenly we had one of those 'mega realisation moments'. The fact was that we hadn't invented a formula, we had discovered it. In checking out the speeches and presentations of outstanding speakers, including Barrack Obama the US president, we could see our formula at the heart of each presentation in its entirety or near so. This startled, delighted and inspired us, all at the same time. A magical moment. Equally, when we watched other presentations by people that lacked something, or were simply plain old boring, we could see that the formula was not being used. And if it had, how that same presentation would have potentially woo'd the audience into adoring submission.

Let's look at the other categories, all of which do have a formula or model. Good movies are based on a tried and tested script model. No model means an awful script. Even if the words are beautifully chosen, the film is just not going to work through lack of structure likes bricks holding up a building. In fact any producer will stop reading the script once it's clear the writer doesn't understand script structure. This also means that some amazing scripts have been created on dull boring topics. Just think about a movie called 'Nine to Five' with an unstructured script. How appealing do you think this movie would have been? The title itself starts to make you yawn. Yet the script is written to a model, and therefore works.

The other thing about a model is that you don't need to know what a great model is to know if one is being used. Audiences vote with their feet and money where movies are concerned and all new movies are screened and tested in front of live audiences. Those movies that get the thumbs down never get into cinemas and are at best relegated to the cheap DVD market.

Plays also have model structures which differ from movies, and songs too have a model structure that when melodious and sung well make millions of dollars for the artist or artistes worldwide. Finally novels definitely have a formula to make them readable.

When people ask:

- 'How do I get the audience to forget everything other than the presentation and focus avidly on what I am presenting?'
- 'How can I gain buy-in from the entire audience, not just a few open minded front seater types?'
- ' What unique things can I do in order to really bond with the audience?'
- 'How do I give the audience such a compelling message that they want to act on it almost straight away?'
- Finally, 'How can I end the presentation with them wanting more?'

The answer lies in having a model sequence to follow that works every time.

Many of our clients are from giant corporations, and we have often been asked to help delegates develop their visuals for strategic conferences. On one occasion, a couple of clients were launching a new product and they'd asked for help with their plenary presentations with an audience of approximately five hundred delegates. The first challenge was helping them elucidate what outcomes they wanted and the second challenge was to actually confront them about their slide deck without bruising sensitive egos. We knew that a few small changes would potentially create a huge positive difference. And the changes were all around the introduction of a presentation model, something they had never considered.

The slide deck was devoid of all structure and took the shape of a casual conversation with the audience. It started with a title slide, went on to making some points, then went back to more about the presenters, a bit about the company then on to the new product, back in time to ten years ago and then it suddenly ended. We looked at each other, then at them, then at the floor. This was enough to strike terror in the faces of our clients who could tell something was desperately amiss.

The first thing about the slides was that the beginning was a non event. But then the rest of it wasn't much better apart from being disjointed and hard to follow. Finally there was no end at all, though this didn't seem to worry them. The short form of what happened next was using the same slides in a different order, plus the addition of a few simple tools and the creation of a strong and powerful ending. Job done. Unsurprisingly, the presentation went down a storm.

Introducing the Alphabet Presenting Model - The Big Picture

The Alphabet Presenting Model is based on A-Z. As already mentioned the first 6 letters A-F cover the 6-Step Presenting model, while the rest of the letters G-Z cover additional tools you may wish to use.

We suggest you always use A-F and then pick 2-3 additional tools from the rest of the letters. Try and avoid always sticking to your favourite additional tools, and try using other alternatives to broaden your experience and expertise. In time you'll become a master presenter because all of it will become subconscious.

You don't need slides to use the model, although slides do help you run the model more successfully when first starting to get used it.

And in any case, a few slides do tend to brighten up a presentation if they are largely pictorial and devoid of unnecessary words. Although we will be exploring the model in more depth in other chapters, let's overview A-F.

Make sure you know A-F really well, back to front, front to back in terms of what the letters stand for.

The A-F Sequence

A is for AGITATE

B is for BENEFITS

C is for CONNECT

D is for DELIVER MESSAGE

E is for EXIT

F is for FOLLOW UP & FEEDBACK

In essence, your presentation should *agitate* the audience in some way. It might be a surprise fact, an unusual opening, starting with something totally unexpected or something controversial. Then to cement the audience to their seats ensure they know the *Benefits* of why they should engage and invest their valuable time. On the subject of engagement, make sure you have *Connected* with the audience. If you haven't, then there's no point going any further until you have done so. If you have connected, you may now *Deliver the Message.*

The *Exit* is the part that most presenters leave out and is like a movie without a satisfying conclusion. Finally there must be some kind of *follow up* and the gaining of *feedback* in order that you, the world-class presenter, can keep honing your skills in the right direction in search of excellence.

It's possible you are reading this and thinking it looks too simplistic. You may even be disappointed hoping the formula was much more complex. But do take heart. Go and watch a top presentation now on YouTube, and provided it's known to have been very successful, you will see ABCDE played out usually in that exact sequence before your eyes.

The world-class in World-Class

Might you still be having an issue with the term *world-class* presenter.

- What is one of these in reality?
- How does this individual come across?
- How would they sound?
- What does it feel like to experience one of their presentations?
- And what's the difference between a world-class presenter and an average one?

Carmine Gallo is a former CNN business journalist and a current columnist for BusinessWeek.com. In his article on the *Presentation Secrets of Steve Jobs,* he listed 10 things that Steve Jobs did to take the accolade of being a world-class presenter, and here they are in Gallo's own words:

1. **Plan in Analogue.** In other words, unlike some of my early customers, keep away from technology initially and create a story board with all of your ideas mapped out. This doesn't matter if you're doing a 5-minute talk, or a 5 day seminar. Do as much in the way of brainstorming as you can.

2. **Create a Twitter-Friendly Description.** If you can't describe your idea, product or service in 140 words, it's time to go back to the drawing board.

3. **Introduce the antagonist or anti-hero.** Jobs always liked to create a villain that allows the audience to rally around the hero, which could be you and your product. The villain doesn't always have to be a competitor, it could be a problem that all of the audience shares and needs a solution for.

4. **Focus on the benefits.** Why should the audience should care about your message?

5. **Stick to the Rule of Three.** Three main messages and no more in your presentation will make it easier to remember, especially if you introduce a way of remembering the message points to the audience.

6. **Sell Dreams not Products.** Jobs used to say: 'For me this is about chunking up your message to a higher level. I can always describe the reasons why I decided to go into business and quite frankly, it was to change people's lives for the better. Many of my business colleagues at the time said they just wanted to pay the bills and I always used to say to them, if you focus people on their own successful personal change, you'll never have to worry about the bills. (It's the same with presenting, when you speak to the audience's heart you really will engage them every single time).

7. **Create Highly Pictorial Slides.** There are no bullet points in Jobs' presentations. Instead Jobs relies on photographs and images. Where the average PowerPoint slide has 40 words, it's difficult to find seven words on 10 of Jobs' slide deck.

8. **Make numbers Meaningful.** Do what you can to assign meaning to any numbers you're using in your presentation. Make sure you put the numbers into context for your audience. For example, in 2009 Apple VP Phil Schiller said that 220 million iPods had been sold to date. He put this number into context at the time by saying that this number represented 73% of the total market.

9. **Use Simple Words in your Presentation.** I love this quote from the ex-General Electric CEO, who said *insecure managers create complexity*. Remove as much jargon as possible and speak simply so any audience can understand you. Because we do so much speaking overseas, I have to keep my English accent as neutral as possible and the words as simple as possible so everyone understands me.

10. **Reveal a 'Holy Smokes Moment'.** This is something in your presentation which is so good, it makes the audience gasp (in a positive, professional way of course!). What can you do in your presentations to make this really happen?

So how do you know you're in the presence of a really top presenter?

A great presenter is the type of person who will always create that 'lean forward factor'. What they're saying and the way the say it elicits such an amazing set of feelings within you that you don't even notice you're leaning forward to capture as much as you can. Blend this with the feeling that all time stands still almost and you suddenly forget where you are, having lost all track of time.

World-class presenters are also the only people who are using a presenting model, and most established presenting superstars are probably totally unaware of this - until they read this book! They are what's termed as unconsciously competent.

When we came up with the concept of *The Alphabet Presenting Model*, we never thought it would have the impact that it has already had on people who have never considered that they could ever call themselves world-class in any sphere, let alone presenting. Yet the before and after videos tell a different and very exciting story. So buckle up and let's throttle up the tempo as we head for the summit of the awe inspiring mountain ahead called *Power Presenter!*

Chapter 3

The Alphabet Presenting Model

In this chapter we are going to focus solely on the 6- Step Structure and really get to grips with why it's so powerful yet easy to use. It will transform any mediocre presentation into something people want to listen to. This being the case just think of the implications of your future presentations based on this model.

Quick test of the A-F Sequence again:

A is for?

B is for?

C is for?

D is for?

E is for?

F is for?

It would be a good bet that you got all of these right as the model does make perfect logical sense when you think about it. But let's drill down in each of these areas in a moment to be clear on the six steps. Each piece of the jig-saw is based on both presenter and audience psychology. It matches what the presenter feels is the right action to take aligned with what the audience expects to receive in turn. Getting these two interfaces connecting is what makes a presenter satisfied to deliver and a delight for the audience member to receive.

A is for Agitate

The word agitate is not used that often. It actually means to disturb, fluster, unnerve, worry or unsettle. It can also refer to shaking, blending, whisking, stirring and churning. None of these appear to be good ideas to open a presentation with; that is until you consider a James Bond movie. This genre of action film has always been famous for agitating an audience at the start, and Bond fans expect a good helping of agitation to get their undivided attention even before the opening credits. Imagine the opposite approach. James Bond appears suited and booted and stands in front of the camera welcoming the audience to the latest adventure. Then proceeds to explain what the plot is and announces the first scene before it begins. What exactly might you be thinking if the very next Bond movie started like this? Might you perhaps be looking at your watch? Squinting for the EXIT sign? And probably reminding yourself of how much money you were parted from a few moments earlier at the ticket booking office. Go to Youtube and check out some Bond movie intros for yourself. See how they engage the audience in seconds.

There are all sorts of time measures for the brain's attention span, but most psychologists agree that 8 minutes would be a fair estimate. If you check out a James Bond movie, you will notice that the first eight minutes or so invariably has you on the edge of your seat. In a presentation the figure is the same, however you will start losing some attention after around 3 minutes if you sound anything less that captivating. This is why a purposeful and practised agitation opening is an absolute must if you want to wow and woo the people listening to you.

You may be forgiven for assuming that the longer the excitement period the better the overall success. Let's think movie again for a moment. If all 120-minutes of a screenplay was agitating, exciting and 'full on' it would surely constitute a great movie, wouldn't it? The reality is that we're much more interested in a roller coaster experience where there are highs and lows rather than being pinned to our seats without any chance of let up until the end. Audiences tend to get a bigger 'kick' if after some agitation they can take a breath and stabilise themselves before the next exciting bit comes along. The A-F part of the model takes full account of this, and in order to kickstart the process well and truly. So to summarise on a good opening agitation is the recommended flame to use on the fuse wire structure of the rest of the presentation. And without taking it to the extreme, anything that disturbs, disquiets or disconcerts in a way linked to your subject, your audience's attention will be captured time after time.

Imagine this as an example. You watch a speaker walk on to the stage looking rather annoyed. She explains that she parked outside the location (she thought) quite legally. Then she produces a parking ticket that she waves in the air to the audience, conveying her absolute dislike for all parking wardens, sharing her negative emotions to many audience members who are nodding empathetically, some wondering if they've also parked in the same place. Her tempo suddenly changes. She pauses, looks carefully at the ticket again in absolute silence. There's a slight pause.

"Oh my God…" she whispers.

You can hear a pin drop. She looks up with a school girl grin.

"Oops", she continues.

At this point everyone in the room is hanging on her every word. Even now as you read these words you may be getting more and more desperate to know how this tale is going to end. Then she reads the ticket to the audience.

"Bring this ticket to the Chicago Pizza Pie Factory today, and we'll give you a pizza of your choice at half price..."

She looks up with a big smile. Maybe there are giggles from the audience as she tosses the ticket aside with joy.

"I'm having a great day today she chuckles. Hope you all are too..."

And then she continues her presentation.

Of course you need to be in the audience to fully get the magic of this agitation opening. In the hands of a speaker who has practised it a few times, the audience will be taken journey of emotions ending their ride in a happy place. Had this same speaker simply come on and said, "Hello, my name is Sheila Davis and I'm pleased to be here today to talk to you about whatever..." it would simply not have had the same impact.

There are various ways you can agitate effectively. These methods include:

- a movie clip

- an unexpected story

- use of an unusual prop brought on stage

- walking on in unusual attire

- extraordinary musical introduction

- an instant magical trick or illusion

- a funny story or joke that you are sure will hit the mark

- an impersonation and so on...

The only limit here is your imagination and the more imaginative you can be the better. Yet there is one rider, and that is, always make it in some way connected or relevant to the overall theme of the presentation. This tip goes for the entire A-F sequence by the way. If any of these 6 elements does not align with the overall message then it's unlikely to be accepted by your audience because it will confuse them.

Imagine the lady with the Parking Ticket was about to talk about, 'The History of the Internet'. She could reference the fact that few marketing initiatives using such a direct approach like a parking ticket on your windscreen ever take this path anymore, and this means either it's less effective or marketers have become lazy.

If however her talk was about, "The Changing Weather in the World", she could then mention the fact that in the future you could park your car and be less worried about getting a ticket and much more worried about whether your car will be still there when you return to it.

However, if you use agitation in complete isolation without referencing your selected subject, you run the risk of looking silly or coming across as plain weird. This would alienate your audience from from the start.

Whether you are making a speech, presenting to colleagues, talking about your holiday, or facilitating a group of business people on a chosen topic, how you start things off matters. If you choose to quietly introduce things in a more traditional manner, it will be quite acceptable but to agitate will get every head and pair of ears squarely focused on you.

With this being the case surely there is only one course of action you can possibly take in the future in opening every time - *agitate!*

B is for Benefits

Given that the overall attention span of an audience is so small from a time perspective, having got their attention from agitation, one needs to hold on to this successful start. Keeping the audience in the palm of your hand you can give them a moment to breathe again from moving on to offering them *Benefits.* If there was a key word to link to Benefits at this stage it would be *tantalise.* Tantalise the audience with up to three benefits. This means it's acceptable to mention just a single benefit or two, but certainly not more than three. Once you go beyond three benefits you run the risk of creating confusion. It's surprising how many speakers who remember to offer benefits at the start of their talks list so many. Worse still they don't confirm that the benefits have been dealt with and served up which may indicate a lack of integrity.

The suggestion for tantalising using Benefits is to choose up to three points and try to find a way the audience will remember them. You could use mnemonics for example. If the subject is: 'Successful French Movies', you could use the word **ACE** which stands for **A**cademy Awards, **C**omedy Films and **E**xtraordinary scenes. You would explain how the audience will get to know what the Top 7 French films of all time are that won awards, (A), why the genre of comedy has often been more successful than thrillers (C). Also what the top grossing French comedies are and sight the most extraordinary scenes ever shot that few of us know about (E). Now if the audience are film buffs they have three reasons to hang around. Imagine you are in this audience.

Is there one of these benefits that has already got your attention? Naturally any benefits you choose should tantalise in the way they're expressed too, including the choice of words that captivate. Getting your 1-3 benefits right will ensure you are on track for a winning presentation, and bear in mind that the fewer the benefits, the more tantalising the benefit listed has to be.

C is for Connect

The next step is *Connecting* with the audience to ensure they really do hear what you have to say with an open mind. If you fail to connect by this stage, or worse - ignore connecting with the audience then you will waste your time from this point onwards as your presentation is likely to be 'dead in the water. Unless the people are truly with you then you may as well be speaking to yourself.

At this connect stage there are two elements at play. Firstly the act of engaging with as many people in the room as possible and secondly, testing the audience that they are fully engaged before going to step 4 which is D for *Deliver your Message.*

There are various things you may do to connect quickly with people, and the most recognised method is eye contact. In a small group of say 2-20 people, there should be no challenge whatsoever to connect eye ball to eye ball with everyone in the room within the first 1-5 minutes. With a larger group, and in particular say 500 people, you would not be able to get eye contact with everyone. In such circumstances the best you can do, which is almost as good, is to make eye contact with individuals in different areas of the room.

This would be done randomly, and although most people will not have had the experience of connecting with you personally, they will be aware that you are doing it with others, which will satisfy them that you are a genuine person at a subconscious level.

The other way to gain a rapid connection is humour, and if this can be reflected towards yourself in some way, it will most certainly win a lot of hearts. This is particularly good to try with British audiences who invariably warm to speakers prepared to poke fun at themselves. You should also consider appropriate body language with open palm gestures and smiles provided it matches the mood of the room. Be careful of smiling in a presentation if the subject is serious and doesn't warrant it.

So to be clear, most powerful connection tools are eye contact and in the UK: self deprecation. Curious how this is not so popular in the US. Here audiences are less interested in feeling a 'lowest common denominator' empathy with the speaker with much more interest in looking up to the person and being inspired or motivated by them. This also signals the fact that you should be conscious of where in the world you are speaking and have done some research regarding the location. For example, Iranian business groups would not want you to mention politics or religion and if you got close to mentioning these subjects you would most likely get people walking out. There was one UK speaker who went to Vietnam to deliver a talk on *The Perception of Money.* Unfortunately, he failed to do his research before hand and nearly became unstuck in the process. During his message, he took out a local bank note and stood on it which caused an immediate stir in the room.

Their bank notes bear images of their current rulers and what he was in fact doing was standing on these people's faces. Whoops! Fortunately they accepted his grovelling apology and saw him as an ignorant foreigner, but his talk received a very low rating and he wasn't asked back.

You could also do a little secret research in the immediately run up to your presentation. Speak to some of the people waiting to hear you if this is at all possible. Ask them what they are hoping to learn or discover, or quite simply the reason they are there in the first place.

If you can then address these things within your talk, you would be tailoring the presentation rather cleverly. If appropriate, mention the people by name when you talk about the issue they raised which gives you more credibility and respect.

The last tip is to think ROI or return on investment. Although most people who listen to you may not have purchased a ticket, they will be making a time investment. For them to leave the room feeling cheated having not gained anything for the time spent will create a feeling of disappointment. The way to deal with this is to ensure each and every presentation has a minimum of 3 valuable 'nuggets' that are shared with the audience. The place that these are best served up is in the next step coming up.

D is for Deliver Message

When running a one or two-day *Power Presenter!* workshop, attendees sometimes assume that this part of the Alphabet Presenting Model, *D for Deliver Message* is simply about giving the audience the main information about your subject matter. Although this is a fair assumption, the way this is done is the key to your success as a 'power presenter'.

Traditionally, presentation skills trainers would talk about your presentation having a 'beginning, middle and end'. In *Power Presenter!* this is inherent in the presenting model, so doesn't apply. Instead think about how food is presented.
Go to one restaurant and order a chilli con carne and you'll get rice on a white plate with a mound of mince and beans at the centre. Go to another more up market cafe and you'll get the chilli in a small pot, the rice in another and then perhaps tiny pots for tacos, mini-peppers and fresh cut salad - all served on an ornate tray. Both are serving the same dish but in totally different ways. The first is a bit traditional and somewhat expected, the other is more non-traditional and largely unexpected. In fact the latter is more of a discovery and therefore exciting.

One speaker decided to link her main points to objects that she placed into a box. For the Deliver part of the model she opened her trunk of goodies and pulled out objects that she referenced to her message. It was certainly unusual and extremely memorable.

In today's media rich society, we expect media to be part of any important message.

Therefore the selection of a YouTube clip or two would go down well, and provided it's sourced live using wi-fi there are no legal issues. Although this sounds complex, it isn't really. Just get the audience to do something for sixty seconds while you go to the clip, then do the same thing after the clip. Or have a helper who goes from your slides to the YouTube clip and back again.

Above all, make your presentation interesting, entertaining and memorable. The bolder the impact, the better the outcome.

E is for Exit

If there was one completely neglected area in presenting skills, it's this one. The most common way people end their presentation is to say 'thanks very much' and then sit down! Yet shouldn't it be the other way around? Shouldn't the audience be shouting, 'Thank-you, thank you!' and then sit down from their standing ovation? Of course standing ovations can be a tough nut to crack, and there are audiences who will not stand under any circumstances. But hopefully you get the idea that ending your presentation must be as dynamic as the beginning of it.

There are great 5 Ways to end or EXIT your presentation. A way to remember them is with the phrase: *The California Class,* or 'THE CA CL'. This helps you remember the five methods:

T - Three Ender

H - Humour

E - Emotion

CA - Call to Action

CL - Close Loop

The Three Ender Exit

You will have seen or heard this many times before. It's a popular choice with politicians, particularly in front of their own party members where a standing ovation is desired.

This exit is based on using a partial sentence, with three different endings to complete the presentation with real panache. A simple version that anyone can use is with the word *Thank you.*

- Thank you for attending today
- Thank you for being so open minded
- Thank you for considering major change in our business

In reality it would sound like this:

"Friends and colleagues, I would sincerely like to *Thank you for attending today,* and *Thank you for being so open minded.* But above all, may I *Thank you* (so much) *for considering these major change in our business..."*

It can of course be a little more sophisticated. Let's imagine the talk is on Major Improvements on Motorways. The way to captivate the audience with 'The Three Ender Exit' is firstly come up with a short sharp snappy 'half sentence' that can be used with three different endings. So for this subject it could be:

"*The Future of Motorways is about....*"

Now consider the three endings. We could have:

1 - co-ordinating positive change for every road user

2 - connecting more people more often

3 - creating a lasting value for generations to come

It could sound like this:

"Friends and Colleagues I'd like to summarise by saying to you that ...*The Future of Motorways is about co-ordinating change for every road user. The Future of Motorways is about connecting more people more often.* But above all, *The Future of Motorways is about creating a lasting value for generations to come.*

There is a definite sound of majesty when you use the 'Three Ender Exit' and it's probably why so many politicians love this as a speech closer.

The Humour Exit

It's well understood that ending a talk on a joke can really complete your message very effectively, but beware of the pitfalls. The most obvious pitfall is do you really want the audience's last recollection of you and your presentation as a joke? Often you will, particularly at weddings, birthdays and other fun events. In business it isn't always an appropriate way to conclude things. This is particularly the case if you want people to go away and consider something important. Having a joke ending merely muddies the waters. Another consideration around humour at the close of a speech is whether it will actually come off as it can be a big risk. What if they don't find your closing comments or story funny?

There have been so many agonising addresses by politicians that are supposed to be funny that hardly get a smile and no doubt the speaker would simply like the ground to open up at this point. Therefore the advice about using a humour exit is:

1 - avoid it in a business presentation

2 - if you use it, make sure your joke, story or comments hit their mark

3 - if in doubt, use another exit

The Emotional Exit

There are many great examples of speeches and presentations that end on an emotional high where both speaker and audience member is reaching for the tissues. The big question is whether such a choice of exit appropriate? Take the address at a rally for insurance sales people. The keynote speaker ends with a story about how he made a sale of critical illness cover to an individual who contracted a serious illness and needed to claim. Subsequently how grateful this person's family were, especially the young children who were able to spend quality time with that person. Well presented, this type of close: 'The Emotional Exit', really does pin people to their chairs. If such a close is appropriate and won't sound overdone or inappropriate, then this can be a powerful way to conclude your talk.

The Call to Action Exit

Used by those wanting to ensure the audience goes away and takes action, 'The Call to Action Exit' is a popular choice by those in the Self Improvement industry. Yet such an exit can be used in any presentation to simply issue a challenge.

You are saying to those listening: "Now you've heard and digested my words, I am asking you to consider going off and doing something about it."

One of the most famous Call to Action Exits was made by Liberal party leader David Steel where he urged colleagues to go back to their constituencies and "Prepare for government". Although it was rather a lame idea based on a small uplift in popularity for the third-placed political party of the UK at the time, it did make a great 'Call to Action Exit', culminating in a lengthy standing ovation.

The Close Loop Exit

The final choice of exit is based on the use of loops. A famous user of loops is British comedian Ronnie Corbett. He would start a funny story then go off and tell other tales before finally coming back to the original story and completing it. Such a technique is easier to do than you may suppose, yet not chosen that often because it does require some thought and preparation. There are also the annoying speakers who commence using this technique, but then fail to close the loop of the original story and the audience go away feeling robbed.

The way you use the exit is to think about the story you wish to use which should be appropriate to the subject matter.

The trick is to be able to begin the story then go off on to another one without someone raising their hands to say, "'Sorry - you never told us what happened on the previous matter…" It can be done with the right story. For example you could tell this story to an audience of seasoned travellers as a Loop:

"Have you ever been on a plane and they dim the lights at night. And have you ever wondered why they do it? I was sitting next to a lady when they made this announcement and she said it was something to do with saving power for the landing gear and landing lights..."

You now leave this story...

"Isn't it true how everyone you travel with has an opinion? It may not be true, but the opinion is shared all the same! The thing about travel I most like is..."

Can you see how you have started a story about aircraft lights and sneakily gone on to something else? What you then do is use the punch line to the initial story as the framework to your EXIT.

F is for Follow Up/Feedback

We looked at ROI or Return On Investment for the audience. Let's flip this for the presenter now. What could be your ROI? If the presentation is about pitching a new idea, influencing with integrity or selling a product/service, then *Follow Up* is vital. There should also be some learning through *Feedback* and these two items would surely be of value to most presenters and make the whole exercise of preparing the presentation, practising the delivery and spending all that valuable time - a worthwhile pursuit.

Follow Up can be as soon as people start to file out of the room, where helpers get e-mail addresses, contact numbers and business cards or that very day by sending out an e-mail. Equally, depending on the desired outcome, the Follow Up can happen a few days later, although certainly no longer than seven. As far as Feedback is concerned, this should be done separately to avoid confusion, and also giving someone a single specific task is better than the expectation that they will give their all on two totally different requests. It would probably be better to get Feedback at the end of the event, or within a few hours by e-mail. If it is to be done in paper form, then make sure the paper is a third of the size of British A4 and that there's no more than 3-5 questions. If it can be tick boxes with a small box for comments, so much the better. Make it easy for the person to comply with your Feedback request rather than sigh at the thought of having to undertake a laborious task, particularly if they are on a high from your superb presentation.

So what do you think of the Alphabet Presenting Model? Could you implement it? Look through this chapter again if needed to make sure you've got it clearly in your mind and most important, test yourself on the A-F so you recall what these letters stand for without much thinking. This is essential before moving on to the next chapter.

Chapter 4

The 3 Presenter Styles

Did you know that there are a limited number of story genres for any movie script? Name any movie and it can be categorised from this list and applies to any country. The same is also true of Presenter Styles and there are in fact only three style types.

Whenever you are listening to anyone addressing a group of people, they are using one or more of these three styles, sometimes blending two styles together, or if they are world-class, they will use all three in the same presentation, to great effect.

The Magic of The Presenter Style

For many people fashion is everything. It's not just choosing clothes for seasonal adjustment to keep your body at the right temperature, its about what you choose to wear, what colours you decide on and what you decide to carry to match the overall image. Despite this, there are those who really don't care what they wear provided the clothes are clean and fit them. These same people never catch people's attention and will invariably blend into a crowd and be part of the masses. It's the same in presentation skills. There are people who think that getting one's words out is all that's needed and that rudimentary basics will suffice. Yet the truth is, style does matter when you communicate or present.

The better quality your output, the more chance you have of being successful in getting your message across successfully. So what are the three styles? The alphabet in the form of ABC may be used again.

A for Actor,

B for Broadcaster

C for Comedian.

As presenters, we all have already chosen one lead style from this list and potentially a secondary style to support our lead style. As you may have surmised looking at the options, the most popular choice is *Broadcaster*. This style is easiest to achieve because it simply requires the speaker to read out or talk without emotion. It's a bit like reading the news. If a news reader started to act out or add comedy to their message, it would completely ruin the intended outcome. But there are times when such a style will be the perfect way to present because it matches the subject or occasion.

A for Actor

When we ask people in *Power Presenter!* workshops to consider adding an acting edge to their presentations, many say they can't act. Actually the Actor Style isn't necessarily about acting, and can be achieved by adding some body language and kinaesthetic texture to their performance. Using your hands more in gestures that better delivers your message *is acting*. So is more body movement, provided that it's not going to distract those watching.

It's also true that many of us are natural actors if we knew it. Remember this is so self evident in children. Where the adult default style is probably Broadcaster, a young child's default style is Actor with a natural leaning to Comedian.

Acting can also be demonstrating what you wish to say by eye contact and subtle facial expressions. The more you be yourself, the greater the chance these natural acting tools surface all on their own.

The reason adults default to Broadcaster is because it feels as if you are more in control, and less likely to make a fool of yourself. Yet by allowing yourself to be who you truly are, and permit personal expressions and body language to permeate your Broadcaster 'body armour', the greater the Actor side of you will emerge. Allowing the Actor Style to flourish will undoubtedly improve your overall image and you will become so much more watchable.

Some instant ideas to be more Actor include:

- use your hands more to express yourself
- make more eye contact
- prepare mini acting sequences and deliver them with confidence
- a change of voice tone when appropriate is acting
- all good acting is based on a 'less is more' philosophy
- ensure there's a story you can 'act out' using gestures and tonality

B for Broadcaster

We have already briefly explored Broadcaster mode, so you may be wondering what else you would need to know.

It's been established that this style can be a default for most presenters, as it appears to offer the maximum control. It's a style that will get the job done and if using a script or any practised presentation, this way of presenting will work.

The downside of sticking with a Broadcaster style is that it can be boring. Okay if you're the president or monarch of a country and millions of people are there to listen to an important message, then no one is likely to expect an actor or comedic style. But sadly for the rest of us, this particular style will become tiring for people, and a classic example of this is the Sunday Sermon at church. (Though it's interesting that some churches are encouraging their representatives to add more acting and humour to Sunday services).

It's important to mention that the Broadcaster style should never be completely eliminated from a presentation because it does have its place and purpose. A good example is world-class speaker Ricky Gervais at one of his gigs in the States. At an award ceremony, he had the entire audience practically on their knees with laughter, and yes he was using acting and comedy, however he would also go into broadcaster style when there was a serious announcement.

This happened right at the start where he introduced himself and what he was there to do and also when it was time to get down to the business of announcing the nominees for the award that he was about to present. But then Ricky Gervais is world-class and what we deem as a world-class presenter is anyone who is comfortable with all three styles, including the most challenging one for most that of *Comedian.*

C for Comedian

It's probably fair to say that most presenters would love to be good at making an audience fall about laughing. It's a great thing to be able to do, and more of us would be able to do this if we had the confidence to pull it off. We also know of people who appear to do this naturally with little or no effort. Certain well known comedians are able to get people laughing just by appearing on stage and looking at the audience. A master of this was the late British comedian, Tommy Cooper. Others with this apparent super ability include Groucho Marx, Joan Rivers, and Benny Hill.

The good news is that we don't need any special talents to add comedy to our presentation. We only need to do the following:

- prepare and practise comedic touches before implementing
- be open to the possibility of live 'instant reaction' quips
- recall and recount real life funny stories that have happened to you

If you can do these three things, you will automatically have a comedy side to your presentations that others might refer to as 'natural' to you! There's a curious fact about many well known 'natural comedians'. Off stage, these very funny men and women are quite sombre, serious and a few even committed suicide. This is a sad observation, yet a fact to support the idea that even professional comedians are probably following the 3 rules as stated above.

Prepare & Practice before Presenting Comedy

One guaranteed way to have a comedy side to your talks is to prepare and practise material. It sounds obvious yet few are happy to go to this length. With the internet you are able to unearth hundreds, if not thousands of jokes, stories and funny tales. Find something that's appropriate and then make it your own with your own words and personal persona. Rather like other points you are going to mention, make sure you know when you will deliver the funny material - and do run it by family and friends if possible before hand. Like most things, the more you practise it, the better it will get. Magicians will attest to the fact that their skill comes from practising many times over.

On average, 10,000 times for a great card trick and 20,000 times for 'slight of hand'. We are not suggesting you should practise so often, but the point is comedy does require a lot of practice in order for it to work effectively.

Be Open to live 'instant reactions'

A great deal of funny things will be said by audience members that happen live during the presentation - totally unrehearsed. There was a moment at a *Power Presenter!* workshop when a male attendee expressed the fact that he was expecting a new member to his family saying: "I'm expecting a baby at the moment". Everyone knew exactly what he meant and no one laughed until the presenter spotted the comedic opportunity and instantly reacted with:

"Does your wife know?"

This of course brought the house down and was of course, very funny. Being open to these opportunities will add comedy to your presentation that is normally funnier than the material you have prepared.

Recall & Recount real life Funny Stories

Millions and millions of dollars are made worldwide by this comedy technique. In the 1960s and 1970s, stand up comedians would come prepared with a variety of jokes that they'd been given or had paid for. Some material would have also been re-worked from classic jokes. Then during the 80s, something changed. Stand up comedians realised that what was much funnier were real stories that preferably happened to them in real life. Provided the story was amusing, they could tell the story and pad it out with other funny comments and ideas to provide a good 10-15 minutes of stand up comedy stage time. A couple of these stories could be their entire act at a comedy gig alongside other comedians. The advice here is to make a list of every funny story you can think of that's happened to you over the years. Keep writing them down as they happen in the present and create an original resource for future presentations.

Blending for Perfection

Although you can get away with choosing a uni-dimensional style to present with, having a blend of two will double the success of your overall performance, and the use of all three styles will quadruple the overall success. You may also want to change your lead style. So if you tend to be a Broadcaster, you may want to lead with Acting from now on. But can you do this? The answer is of course and it's very straight forward. To start with you must be certain what the style is going to be and be clear why you want to change it. Comedian Clement Freud used to have a dead pan yet droll Broadcaster lead style which got him lots of work. Had he changed it to Actor style, he would have been less amusing.

Nevertheless, if change is what you want, once you know what that new style is, with lots of preparation and planning, lead with it for the next 6 presentations. After that, rest assured it will be your new lead style.

Style Improvement Tips

1. Choose Other Styles on Purpose

Force yourself to do other styles on purpose. You may be great at Acting and Comedy, but make yourself do Broadcaster in your presentation and see what effect you have been missing out on.

2. Practise Your Weak Style

Whatever your third (or reluctant) style is, this is most likely to be your 'weak style'. Yet it's only weak through lack of use. Like a muscle that is not used much it can waste.

3. Use 'Magic Bullets' for All 3 Style Options

We will be exploring the concept of Magic Bullets. (In the G-Z Tools see M for Magic Bullets). Using this approach by having a magic bullet for each of the three styles will make you more confident to use each style.

4. Use Youtube to Learn about Styles

YouTube has thousands of presentations uploaded, and of course presenters using the ABC styles in differing formats. A good place to start is to review TEDX talks, and in particular, those with the highest number of hits and likes.

5. Start & Finish with 'Broadcaster' Style

A very safe way to add style and control to a presentation is to start and finish with Broadcaster style. This is most recommended if you lack confidence.

Knowing you have a strong confident opening and exit means few fewer risks with the presentation between these step points.

6. Two vs Three Styles

Finally, if you had to choose between being great using just two styles or good using all three, then of course you go for two! However, getting too comfy sticking to two styles is probably laziness and you should explore your missing style and do as much as possible to incorporate it so that you can evolve as world-class.

Chapter 5

Gestures and Body Language

As previously alluded to, there are two types of people: those who brighten up the room when they enter it and those who brighten up the room up when they leave it. You know what it's like being around the former because they really leave you with a positive feeling. Think of somebody right now who brightens up the room when they enter it. Identify them in your mind. Are they a relative, friend or work colleague? It doesn't matter for now who you have chosen as long as you can see them in your mind's eye. Notice what they're doing to brighten the room up, as if it's going on right now. Hear what they're saying to convey their positive message, be aware their tone of voice and notice how it makes you feel. In fact, think about where that sensation starts and where it moves to as these people tend to leave you with a sudden rush of excitement that can last for a very long time. You tend to feel energised, uplifted and ready to act in a different way as a result of this interaction.

Someone who does this for many audiences is motivational speaker, Les Brown. You don't even have to see him or be in the same room as him to feel him brightening up your mood.

Sometimes all you need to do is put on one of his audios and that's enough. His energy is contagious and you can't help but feel great once you've listened to him speak.

Les Brown is the complete antithesis of the mood hoover or psychic vampire, as the terms go. These other people seem to have an innate ability to suck the energy out of you so that you feel drained, sometimes frustrated and often irritated in their presence.

Now you'd hope that any presenter would put themselves in the former category and yet watching people present will make you realise that there are things that world class presenters subconsciously do that give their audiences the energy they need to act on the positive messages that they've seen, heard and felt. This compares significantly with the average presenter who at best will brighten the room up fleetingly by luck, or at worst leaves the audience wondering why they even bothered attending in the first place. Not good.

Although you may be thinking, this is more positive thinking hype isn't it? It's actually far more significant than that. Sometimes you may have to deliver news to a group of people that's not so positive and the way you deliver it will most certainly impact the outcome, which surely matters a great deal. Do you want the audience up in arms or in total rapport, empathy and conscious understanding? It's about the things we can do to excite and enthuse our audience without even speaking to them, as well as what we can avoid doing to make sure that the audience is subconsciously on our side. So we'll be looking at the significance of your mindset, how you use your hands, legs, feet and eyes, plus the importance of 'personal congruence' and use of your whole body when connecting with an audience. We'll also look at what World Class Presenters do instinctively and how all this will make a difference in your future presentations.

The Importance of Your Mindset

Your mind is a powerhouse of potential in terms of what it can do. Neuroscientists have only scratched the surface in terms of discovering its total natural ability and ever aware that research results means revising accepted scientific understanding. Even when we're sleeping, our mind is still hard at it, working away regardless. How many times have you said to yourself:

"I have a really important meeting tomorrow and I must get up at 6.00 am".

You set your alarm and think, "I really hope I wake up in time". The next morning at 5.55 am, you become your own alarm and you're awake and ready to go. Think about this. The human mind is so incredible that just the mere suggestion of you needing to wake up by a certain time will alert your subconscious mind, the 'invisible butler' to program you to wake up. This is just one incredible thing your mind is able to achieve if you just allow it to work naturally. Presenting is another.

So to re-cap we know that the human mind has two facets that help us with our decision making on a day to day basis, namely the conscious mind and the subconscious mind. If we consider consciousness is anything we're aware of, then for example if you were asked to think about your chin all of a sudden your chin becomes part of your conscious awareness. Your chin was always there it's just that you weren't thinking about it until it was mentioned.

An experiment was carried out in 1956 by one of the founders of the field of cognitive psychology George Miller which led to the paper 'The Magical Number Seven, Plus or Minus Two'.

This related to the fact that based on his observations, Miller calculated that a human being's short term memory capacity, (in other words the ability to consciously remember information) equated to the number 7 +/- 2. This piece of information is incredibly important when you think about what it is you'd like your audience to remember. Both when you present to them as well as how much information you should be placing on a visual aid at any given time. Done well, you connect, amaze, entertain and get your message across well. So often it isn't done well and in truth there's no excuse. What's even more exciting than George Miller's experiment is all the work that's been carried out to determine what's possible in your subconscious mind. We've already discussed your biological alarm clock capability and yet there's so much more to your unseen mind. In fact many authors on neuroscience state that the subconscious mind has the ability to process around 2 million pieces of information through our senses a second. But what's the connection with making fantastic presentations?

Let's look at how we process information below our consciousness and the impact it can have from the presenter's view as well as that of the audience.

Our brain relies on our senses to bring it information, while our sensory experiences are converted into a picture, a sound or a feeling inside our minds. These sensations are then run through a series of filters that handle memories, attitudes and values. Next our filters pass these pictures sounds and feelings into an even more powerful analysis system that deals with distortion, deletion and generalisation. You see, without mental filters we would be overwhelmed with the amount of information that the brain receives; potentially 2 million pieces per second.

Audiences Distort, Delete and Generalise

These filters help us make sense of information, yet can be 'deadly' for any presenter. Lack of clarity can *distort* information. *Distortion* is when the brain twists the information into a 'truth' in order to make it make more sense. That's why in a crime, witnesses claim to have seen evidence that bear no semblance to reality, yet under oath they are convinced otherwise. Imagine having your message completely distorted by an audience who have been fed the wrong information by how you look, what shoes you have chosen to wear, or the choice of words which are inappropriate for a particular culture or audience. *Distortion* could be when you attach meaning to something that someone has said or done. How many times have you greeted someone and for some other reason, they haven't greeted you back.

It's very likely you'll start drawing negative conclusions about your relationship believing they don't like you anymore or you've done something to upset them. A distortion of reality. It happens all the time.

Deletion is another potential spanner in the works. Take a foreign looking woman from South America who tells a story of when she was visiting Malaysia, then at the end of her presentation she someone asking her how many of her family still live in Kuala Lumpa. Now what's happened here is that people have picked up her foreign appearance and Malaysia and deleted the part where she mentions she's from Brazil. When you delete information you do so because it's not perceived as relevant or doesn't fit with your beliefs.

How many times have you walked down the same road, believe you recognise all the buildings on that road and then see what you believe is a new shop, until someone tells you that the shop has been there for 5 years. It's easily done and happens because your brain didn't think that particular shop was relevant. It 'deleted' the building from your mental map.

Finally that pain creating filter called *Generalisation*. This can be quite embarrassing too. Like going up to an overweight woman and asking when her baby is due. You have made a generalisation about a female with a bit of a belly, equating it to pregnancy.

Or that well known story of a boy taken to hospital with a fractured arm in a car accident where his father who was driving the car was still at the scene with two broken legs. Yet as he's wheeled into the operating theatre the surgeon exclaims, " I can't operate. He's my son!" This floors most people until you explain the surgeon is his mother. Alas, generalisation is still rife in politics, ethnicity, sexual preference and corporate board rooms all over the globe. Generalisation helps us learn from previous experience, otherwise every time you approached a new design for a door for example, you would spend a long time working what it was exactly since it did not match your understanding of what a door is supposed to look like. The challenge with generalisations is that our learning experiences are not just related to new door designs.

If you've had a bad experience, such as a business partner who was dishonest with you, it's possible for you to believe all potential business partners are dishonest and that could be an over-generalisation that isn't of course always true. So the process of generalising is neither good nor bad but how you use it could be.

Getting back to gestures and body language. As humans we have an amazing propensity to be able to tell what people are thinking by reading their body language, provided we pay attention.

Of course many audiences do so subconsciously and if the presenter is not switched on, poor gestures and uncertain body language, with the combination of distortion, deletion and generalisation can create mayhem in the minds of the audience, which is a complete misrepresentation of the naive presenter. Let's develop this concept a bit further with some work highlighted by the well respected and celebrated author Malcolm Gladwell in his book 'Blink: The Power of Thinking without Thinking'.

Gladwell's *Thin Slicing* and how it applies to Presenting

Malcolm Gladwell asserts that 'Thin Slicing' is all about our subconscious mind being able to predict the future based on very narrow experiential content analysis at lightening speed. Have you and your friends met another friend who has a new partner who have declared their intention to marry, yet you and your friends have that side conversation expressing your skepticism as something in your gut tells you something's not quite right about the relationship? Happens a great deal. Where does that shared gut feeling come from?

There's also John Gottman who is famous for his work on marital stability and divorce prediction who took thin slicing to a new level when he developed the 'The Love Lab'. John and his co-workers interviewed over three thousand married couples in a small room near the University of Washington. Each of the couples were videoed having a conversation, with electrodes and sensors attached to their fingers and ears measuring such things as heart rate and temperature.

The couples also had another monitor to see how much each of them moved around on their chairs. Gottman and his team created a coding system with 20 separate categories linked to every possible emotion that each married couple might express during the conversation. The team members were all trained on how to read and interpret the micro movements displayed by each of the couples and all of this information was fed in to a computer. Being able to watch an hour of video footage on a couple allowed Gottman and his team to predict with 95% accuracy whether the couple would still be married fifteen years later. If only 15 minutes of the video was watched the success rate fell to 90%. Indeed, one of Gottman's colleagues was able to predict accurately with just three minutes of video footage.

Gottman's experiment obtained some tremendous results and yet thin slicing is something we do a lot of the time. Our subconscious mind is primed to use this process at lightening speed to protect us. We tend not to call the process thin slicing we normally associate this with instinct or gut feel, and we are very good at it.

Isn't it amazing how we can meet someone for the first time and immediately take a liking to them as if they are a long lost friend and then on the other hand we can meet another person and the theme music to 'Jaws' suddenly starts playing in our head and we are wary of this person. Many people allow their conscious mind to override gut feelings and when things go wrong there's that reflection that they should have trusted their gut instinct in the first place.

Now imagine being able to affect thin slicing from the start. Being able to give a good positive feeling to your audience as they thin slice you from every which way. This is why gestures and body language are critically important, and by following a few simple rules that are exceptionally easy to perform, you win in every presentation, every single time. It also enhances the energy between the presenter and the audience and starts with the signals we emit by the way we use our hands, legs, feet and eyes.

Hand Gestures

There are so many ways that our hands can either help or hinder in building strong associations in the minds of our audience. People often wonder what to do with their hands when presenting. Here is some hand related non-verbal communication to avoid:

The Windmill Position

This is when your arms are all over the place like a windmill, which can be tiring for your audience and will most certainly deflect from the key messages you're wanting to get across.

Jangling Money or Keys in your Pockets

Do people actually do this anymore? Yes they do, and it's even worse if they don't have any money or keys in their pockets.

The Royal Family Position

Think Prince Charles with his hands behind his back in a rather regal stance. Works for Charles but it's unlikely to be a winner for you. It may even come across as a bit arrogant.

The Preacher

Speakers clutching a lectern will often remind an audience of a member of the clergy perched at the pulpit. Is this the association you want to give to the audience? Even religious speakers will probably want to avoid this at all costs.

The Fig Leaf Position

This looks as if the speaker is expecting a direct free kick in a soccer match or standing with his or her hands protecting the crotch area which always seems slightly strange when presenting. If the person then opens up their hands it's often unkindly referred to as the 'Fig Leaf Flasher' technique.

Folded Arms

You've seen this before where the speaker has their arms folded while speaking to the audience. Typically body language specialists will tell you that we do this when being defensive and the folded arms are nature's way of helping us to protect our vital organs!

So what do you do with your hands?

There are five distinct patterns of non-verbal communication that are specific postures that involve the entire body, including your hands. These are called *Satir Category Patterns,* named after Virginia Satir who was an eminent psychologist. One of the things that she noticed during her family therapy sessions was that during their discussions, her clients would display certain stances that could help or hinder the connection with their family when they were in the same room.

These stances, of which there are five, became known as the Satir Categories and they are movements of the hands which normally happen subconsciously, and yet, when used with positive intention and integrity, will enhance your communication style. The stances work across all cultures. They are known as:

- The Leveller
- The Placater
- The Blamer
- The Computer
- The Distracter

The Leveller

In this position you, as the speaker will have symmetrical physiology. Upright, moving hands, palms down, in a levelling movement that's spreading.
Subconsciously you're telling the audience: *This is the way it is* and *this is true.*
With the Leveller your voice has a falling tonality, and you are slowing down as you action the movement. The Leveller asserts authority and calms people down, so it's good for bringing things down to earth.

Using the falling tonality and pauses also makes a big difference. When might you see this in a presentation? Normally when you are giving factual information that may have a serious undertone to it. This could be information that you may want the audience to take a note of such as your key message.

The Placater

In this position we can see symmetrical open physiology from the presenter.

Palms up, moving in an upward direction and subconsciously you're telling the audience: *I'm open* and *I want to please you*. The Placater suggests openness and even some vulnerability. This signifies agreeing with everything, is talking in an ingratiating way, and is always trying to please. When would you use this? Perhaps at the beginning of a presentation when you're looking to have the audience on your side. Another time could be when you're dealing with challenging questions from an audience.

The Blamer

The Blamer has an asymmetrical stance, leaning forward, and pointing their finger. "It's your fault", "It's down to you."

The blamer comes from a position of superiority and is more interested in throwing their weight around. It is unlikely that you would use the full blamer posture when presenting. Rather than use one finger, use two fingers together or your fingers in a beak shape which is less confrontational. The blamer brings life to a presentation when you're pushing a point home, to literally punch the key points of your message.

"There are 3 points I want you to get. The first point is... the second point is..."

You are adding emphasis, indicating what matters, while telling your audience that it concerns them. One effective way of using it is with the phrase:

"You can do it," pointing to individuals in the audience.

The Computer

This is another asymmetrical stance. Hand on chin or arms folded like a 'thinker' pose, the message here being conveyed to audience is:

I'm the authority', I'm reasonable logical and sensible and *here are the facts. Judge for yourself.*

It's likely you would use 'The Computer' in situations when you want to communicate *I'm thinking about what you said..."*

Go into Computer mode if someone asks you a question, and you need a little time to answer it.

The Distracter

The final Satir Category, 'The Distractor', shows asymmetrical physiology. Angular, disjointed and incongruent .You're saying to the audience:

I simply don't know and *It's not my fault.*

It's the classic: 'Don't Shoot the Messenger Posture'.

When would you use this? Not very often, as it can, as the name suggests, be a real distraction and even annoying if used often. This stance is great for distracting hecklers as the accusations just bounce off.

Putting the Stances Together

In a group, try these Satir Categories for yourself.

- Adopt the posture, add the gestures, and say some of the typical sentences using the relevant tonality. Notice the change in your state as you do it.
- Have someone else do each category in front of you, so that you become familiar with being on the receiving end, hearing that voice tonality and seeing that type of physiology.
- Each group writes a sketch where you use all of the categories and assign someone to present back.
- The other group guesses the categories and notices changes in physiology and tonality and the effect on them.

This will really help you to understand what each category looks like as well as the context within which it is used.

So we've looked at what not to do with your hands as well as what tends to happen naturally when you're presenting. The number one tip that we can give you about your hand positioning is to simply keep your hands above your waist line. It's what we refer to as the *Neutral Position*. If you do this your hands will naturally follow your words and gestures. Ideally place one hand into the other or simply link them loosely together. If you want to further explore what professional presenters and TV people do with their hands, check out news reports.

Most are no longer carrying microphones. Observe how each presenter will have their own favourite neutral position that they use often from time to time and certainly go back to.

Using your Hands and Feet to Mark out Time

Just for a moment in your mind's eye think of a time when you brushed your teeth five years ago and point to where you might represent it in front of you in mid-air. Now think of a time when you brushed your teeth a year ago and point to where you represent it in the same way. Now think of brushing your teeth in the present moment right now and point to where that is. Now think of a time one year in the future when you need to brush your teeth and point to where that is. Finally imagine brushing your teeth 5 years in the future and point to where that's represented. Now draw an imaginary line from five years ago right through to the present day and on to five years in the future. This is your *timeline*.

It's likely that when you worked out your timeline you either represented in one of two ways. Either your past was behind you, the present is inside you and the future is in front of you and this is known as *in-time* or the past was to your left the present is straight in front of you and the future is to your right and this is referred to as *through-time*.

This is significant when you're presenting in a couple of very important ways. If you can imagine the area where you are presenting is a stage and your audience is in front of you, it's possible to mark out time using your hands and feet and marking out an imaginary timeline going from stage left to stage right, in other words creating a through-time analogy on the stage.

It would be more of a challenge using the in-time analogy here, as you then have to cope with the depth of the stage. If you imagine the stage where you're presenting is like a television screen and you're on television then you can see that you have the whole width of the audience's imaginary television screen to play with. The simple advice is think mirror image and your audience will understand your message.

Using you Feet Effectively

Just to keep this really simple, there are two things to say where feet are concerned. The first is wear appropriate clean footwear when presenting and use your feet to move only when you need to move.

Firstly it's amazing how many people tend to look others up and down and register what people are wearing and so many presenters have dirty shoes who stand up and present in front of hundreds of people.

The second point is to consider how much you move your feet when presenting. If you're constantly moving your feet as you talk, and you've probably seen people do this rhythmic dance with their feet, it can be so distracting and also look ridiculous. It may be only a small movement, like rocking from left foot to right foot side to side or backward and forwards, but it's still bad news. Some people do a more elaborate movement as if they're doing some kind of 1970s formation dance routine. When its mentioned it to the presenters what's astonishing is that they didn't even know they had done it.

Moving your feet from time to time is a good thing or you look too statue like, but in doing so let it be for a reason such as marking out time on your 'stage' or moving to a specific point new place to stand with purpose.

If you have a challenge in keeping still, one technique I suggest is to stand up with a chair resting against your legs, this gives you a 'prop' to help stay still until you need to move to emphasise a point or mark out time. An alternative is sitting on a bar stool which will definitely keep you from moving.

"Eyes are Mirrors to the Soul"

We have already mentioned eye contact but it's so important, here's some more. How many times have you been part of an audience where the presenter only spoke to a fraction of the group? This is very irritating, especially if the presenter has taken the time to ask the whole audience a question, you've put your hand up to answer and then he or she ignores you completely. Breaking rapport with your audience is a cardinal sin and can transform a supportive group into a hostile crowd.

Eye contact is one of the best ways to create rapport and engage an audience right from the start. It allows you to offer positive energy to the audience that is likely to be swiftly reciprocated. The most important tip when it comes to eye contact is to include the entire room. But how do you do that? Well here's a little exercise you can do the next time you're in front of a group of people who are prepared to experiment.

Maybe at a team meeting or with a group of friends. Take it in turns to stand up in front of the group and your main objective is to make sure that you connect with everyone in the group at pretty much the same time. As the presenter, the way that you will be able to tell whether you've connected with each individual and therefore the group as a whole, will be the fact that each person will put their hand up as soon as they feel like they've been included by you as you look in their direction.

As an audience member, you're looking for the presenter to connect with you directly and feel as if for a tiny moment in time that person is connecting with you to the exclusion of everyone else in the room.

What you'll notice is that as soon as you the presenter at the front looks at an audience member and both of your gazes meet, you'll have an instant connection. This is confirmed if you smile and they smile back. You'll also notice that if your gazes meet and your audience member doesn't lift their hand, a gentle raise of the eyebrows usually does the trick as raised raised eyebrows is a subtle way of saying *over to you!* Therefore you are making a gentle suggestion that it's the other person's turn to reciprocate.

Eye contact is also great to help you put your thoughts together, have clarity of thought and also to help you to remember what you're supposed to be saying. Remember your goal is to connect with individuals in the room. Connecting with them is a double edged sword because if you spend too long looking at one person in the audience it can be really intimidating for that person, also if you spend too little time with an individual they will be likely to disconnect.

If you're running a training session for say twelve to fifteen people, and you have the chairs arranged in a U-shape, it's easy to work with a small group at one side of the room and slowly make your way with your eyes to the other side of the room in a systematic fashion. The best tip here is to spend one sentence at a time with one person, once you're about to move on to the next sentence or phrase, move on to the next person.

When you're looking at people, look at their eyes not directly into them, otherwise it could give a signal that you may not want to give, especially when engaging someone in the audience of the opposite sex.

In very large audiences no one expects a presenter to make eye contact with everyone, yet everyone feels positive about a presenter who makes every effort to make eye contact with as many people as is possible in the time available. However it is possible to split up the room into sections and start with making eye contact with people at the front of the room, then work your way to the back. From there move to the side of the room and finally, the other side. When you speak to one section of people at a time, each individual will feel like you're speaking with them directly.

The Importance of Congruence

What is congruence? In power presenting it's *agreement, harmony, balance and equilibrium.* Personal congruence when presenting is so important. Personal congruence refers to a state in which a person's values and beliefs are consistent with the way he or she lives their life.

One main reason why personal congruence is so crucial when presenting is that it stops you sending out the message, or signals to the audience that you're somehow a fake. The relationship between you and your audience is based on trust and if the audience in any way thinks that what you're saying doesn't match up with your actions then they won't listen to what your saying.

The 8 Signs You and Your Audience Know You are Congruent.

1. There's nothing mysterious about you. People know who you are.

2. You have clear goals that are transparent to your audience.

3. You are aware of your shortcomings and mention them to your audience to help them build a connection with you. Self Deprecation also creates strong rapport.

4. You deal with fears and look fearless when presenting.

5. You use positive self-talk avoiding unhelpful phrases or words during your presentation, such as, *can't, unfortunately, unable, difficult* and *problem.* Plus cliches, such as *in the final analysis* and *to be honest.* Words and phrases that can easily break rapport with your audience.

6. You express personal emotions so people know where they stand with you, although anger is always inappropriate, unless you're telling a story.

7. You're organised and the audience feel in safe hands.

8. Finally, you're happy to ask for help and opinions from the audience.

So what if you currently feel like you lack a few of the eight points when you're presenting, what can you do to build yourself up to having personal congruence? Do the following exercise at least once a day in your imagination over the next few weeks and notice what a difference it makes to you as a presenter.

The Three Questions

Every audience is looking for you to fulfil three main questions in their mind as they listen to you.

- Do you like me even though I may have differing views?
- Do you respect me and my presence?
- Do you value me being here listening to you?

Answer these with the right gestures and body language and notice the great results that follow.

Chapter 6

Adding Humour

Despite rumours to the contrary, the idea of adding fun and merriment to your presentation is much easier than you may ever suppose. In this chapter we will tell you how to achieve this with minimum fuss and effort, but also expand upon tools and techniques to make sure you can go as far you desire in making people laugh when you want them to. We have already covered three simple ways to enter the comedy arena in Chapter 4. They are again:

- *prepare & practise*
- *be open to live 'instant reactions'*
- *recall & recount real life funny stories.*

Eighty percent of humour will still relate to doing these three things really well. Now we are going to look at the other twenty percent of the comedy formula, which will sky rocket you into the professional stand-up comedy arena.

Like movie genres, there are only about 10 types of jokes in the world. This is often a big surprise to many. You are probably wondering how this can be with so many jokes out there.

But like songs, screenplays, poetry and art, the types of joke structure are limited and this is good news because it means it's far easier to master comedy knowing it has small boundaries.

The 10 Most Common Joke Types

1 - Logical Ambiguity

Let's start with the most common type of joke. The structure of this funny offering is known as *Logical Ambiguity*. It's based on something that makes perfect logical sense, then extending this logical accepted fact a step further, taking the logic to a farcical outcome. Let's look at an example.

Logical Ambiguity Joke

I have two relatives on my wife's side of the family who always used to go to Brighton for their holidays. In fact they had been doing this for over 20 years and even went to the same hotel. Then my wife asked me to help them broaden their horizons - which I did. It took me 6 months of brain washing. And one Sunday afternoon they rang me with the good news. They were going to Portugal for their holidays! We were delighted for them, they were over the moon. (Pause) That was nine years ago... and ever since (slight pause)... they've been going to Portugal every year for their holidays!

The reason this invariably gets a laugh is because it's based on pure logic, plus empathy for the type of person who hates change.

What a great joke if your talk was also about people hating change. Tommy Cooper loved to use Logical Ambiguity. Here are a couple of his Doctor classics.

TOMMY: Doctor I keep thinking I'm a dog.

DOCTOR: Then lie on the couch so I can examine you

TOMMY: But Doctor, I'm not allowed on the couch.

Now imagine the body language of Tommy fending off lots of women with his hands:

TOMMY: Doctor I have these dreams of women chasing me - and I keep pushing them away. Seriously Doctor. Chasing me - and I keep pushing them away...

DOCTOR: What do you expect me to do about it?

TOMMY: Break both my arms.

2 - The Surprising Anti-Euphemism

Often we use a euphemism to cover up a more blatant word. Yet when an audience are lulled into a sense of false security expecting the euphemism to be used, and then instead get the blatant word - it becomes funny!

Surprising Anti-Euphemism Joke

Our window cleaner's getting on a bit. Been with us for years. Meticulous... cleans every window. Peeks right in sometimes looking for smears on each pane. Doesn't hold back regardless whether it's the kitchen, bedroom, even bathroom. Our window cleaner's one of a kind. (Pause) The Perverted Kind!

3 - The Question + Extreme Answer

This is where a question is asked by the presenter and the answer is also given by the presenter, or a question is asked in a story situation and the answer is delivered by another character in the story. The stimulus for humour is where the answer is as extreme as it gets. The complete opposite of what you are expecting the answer to be...

The Question + Extreme Answer Joke

And there we were, Mikey and me at three o'clock in the morning walking down this dark pokey corridor completely drunk out of our skulls and suddenly we see this bright light... then from the light steps the shape of this small slim woman with her hand outstretched pointing to my wallet. Mikey asks: "Who is that?"
I took a closer look and shouted back: "Well it isn't Mother Theresa!"

4 - The Pun (Paronomasia)

This is a well known joke type that's a form of play on words giving a word two meanings at same time. This joke structure will often attract a laugh followed by a groan at the same time, not because it's that funny, more because it's rather clever and fits!

The Pun Joke

*Yes... sleeping out under the stars is my new hobby. I simply love it. And the thing I love most about Camping is that **its intense.** (In tents).*

5 - Extreme Euphemism

As you know, a euphemistic word is a harmless word in place of something frightening, offensive or unspeakable. Sometimes when you use a euphemistic word or expression to purposely mask the real thing it can be quite funny. The classic example is telling a horrific story about your sixteen year old son who survives a plane crash then you refer to it euphemistically as 'a character building exercise'.

The way this works in reverse is where you would expect to use a soft fluffy expression then flip it for something stronger/extreme on purpose.

Reverse Extreme Euphemism Joke

Taking my loveable elderly grandma through security at an airport is sadly no walk in the park. It has to be done with respect and care. Half her limbs are made of titanium with sophisticated electronic circuitry to keep her heart going. Some say she's an accident waiting to happen. I say she's a danger to terrorists.

6 - Funny Figures

Most people know that surveys can say just about anything you want them to. This becomes amusing when you make a point through the figures you're sharing. For example, what polling university students on sexual promiscuity.

Funny Figures Joke

Surprising results from a survey of 100 university students who were polled on sexual promiscuity. 10 percent said it was a sin. 30 percent said they were not promiscuous at all and waiting for the right person to come along. A massive 51 percent said they had considered multiple partners but hadn't made up their minds yet. And 9 percent said it was totally unacceptable. Promiscuity was a big mistake that was eating into tuition fees now they had several young children to support.

7 -The Understatement

As you read through these comedic structures you will see that 'extremes' are a funny tool that's used quite often.

The Understatement when delivered with subtlety or sarcasm can be extremely funny. Oscar Wilde was a master of this form of humour. Top stand-up comedians use it all the time. It's about playing down something that would ordinarily be played up...

The Understatement Joke

My wife was driving when the car broke down. She was determined to show she could do anything that I could in such circumstances, and I didn't want to spoil her delusion.

As she was wielding the tools from the toolkit she dropped the jack on my foot and I was hopping around in agony. She asks meekly, "Are you alright love?"

"I'm fine", I said. "I'm just trying to attract the attention of a passing emergency vehicle".

8 -The Surprise Person

You're telling a story about someone you met. Nothing seems funny about the interchanges until you finally reveal who the person is and the person's identity is a total surprise.

The Surprise Person Joke

Ok, I admit it. I have a problem. So I confided with a friend and he said he'd help. We ended up in this lap dancing club. He and I are very close by the way. He's been a confident since I was a teenager. Then guess what... I noticed he was finding the experience also very exhilarating. (Pause) Which is a concern ...given he's my priest.

9 - Asking the 'Flaming Obvious'

You are watching an advert on TV for beer. The product is for beer that you re-name 'Golden Nectar'. Now you can use this story at your next presentation by asking rhetorical questions…

Asking the 'Flaming Obvious' joke

So I was watching this advert of TV. Clever things adverts. In short, they work, but why do they work? I mean some are quite ridiculous. Like the advert for Golden Nectar. (Q1) Golden Nectar? (Q2) Where do they get these names from? (Q3) Do they lock advertising execs in a small room with only beer to drink and no loo? (Q4) And they only get freed if they come up with a brand name PDQ? (Q4) I mean how can it be 'Nectar?' (Pause) It's flaming beer for goodness sake! And hardly golden. (pause) Well maybe it is after you drink it!

10 - Set Up and Punch

Classic joke structure as old as time itself. Here you tell a story which is leading up to a punch line. Very straight forward structure. Normally the punch line is something that the listener is simply not expecting.

When considering adding humour to a presentation we suggest you avoid trying too hard. Less is always more, and do try and pick up live opportunities to make light of something, with the exception of the audience! Unless of course you are absolutely sure no offence will be taken. Better to make yourself the butt of jokes.

Chapter 7

The Power of the Story

Imagine a world with no stories. Seriously, consider that either the government has banned all forms of stories or you've woken up in a sort of twilight zone where stories never existed. What would a world devoid of stories look, feel and sound like? There would be no need for television other than factual material, the cinema would simply be an extension of television output, the theatre would be for musicals only where lyrics would be meaningless, and there certainly would be few keynote speeches that inspire audiences to a standing ovation.

Stories are in fact the number one product since cave dweller times. These homes would be adorned with sketches of what hunting was about and how they survived against sabre toothed tigers and the like. All of this illustrated in visual story format; probably the first storyboards ever. And so throughout the centuries, kings, queens, men women and children have all revelled in wanting and needing stories to brighten their lives and sometimes distract them from the worry of where the next meal would come from. The first amazing stories that mankind is aware of are probably the ones etched on the walls of the El Castillo cave in Cantabria, Spain and these are approximately 40,000 years old.

Good stories have also always been a sought after commodity throughout history. Today soaps are a major user of the story mechanism and this story genre now span decades.

The the UK *Coronation Street* started in the early 60s and over fifty years later the story still continues. It's rather like life itself where players in the story may fade and die but 'the powerful play goes on' and never reaches an ultimate conclusion. Any great story will start as a seed in the mind of the conceiver, then sprouts shoots and potentially grows in the mind of the receiver. If it's half good, it will also make a lot of money for the originator. If you need proof ask Stephen King or J.K.Rowling.

Now think about an important presentation completely devoid of a story spine. Why would any presenter not want to have a story to hang their presentation on? Indeed a main story with little off shoot stories would work exceptionally well. Of every 100 presentations that happen each day in sales, team meetings, product launches and group communications, a staggering 68% will feature no story at all. A further 19% percent will have a few token stories that have not been fully thought through and only 3% will be 'power presentations' using the story to its full extraordinary capacity. This is quite shocking isn't it?

A Story from Chris Cummins

Just over a decade ago, I was preparing for a sales conference. As a senior sales manager,it was my role to create the atmosphere for positive motivation and a call to action for the sales team to dig deep and sell more. I was being asked as a manager to inspire them to do this. I prepared my presentation in the way I'd become accustomed which was to ask our production company to create a 90 plus Power Point slide show replete with bullet points, statistics, percentages and other tasty morsels (not). One of my bosses, a director of the company posed an interesting question:

"Chris, why do you need all these slides? I know that you're good at telling stories. All you need to do is to tell the team an inspirational tale from the heart in your usual enthusiastic manner and this alone will do the trick… they will go away inspired to sell more, I guarantee you. I smiled broadly, not realising my boss was serious, so I continued to ignore similar hints for the next… few years!

So what was holding me back from making this transition from 'slide jockey' to inspiring storyteller? Well it was a poor belief I was hanging on to. And we all know that if you spell belief out loud there's an LIE at it's centre. Potentially all beliefs have a lie at their centre. The lie I was telling myself was that business presentations are a serious matter. You mustn't have fun with them because you might entertain the audience too much. They will love what you're saying to them and where would that lead to? Exactly! I'd have to make every presentation entertaining and engaging, and that would never do.

I'm delighted to say that this story has a happy ending. I once forgot to load my slide presentation in the car and found myself in front of 50 hungry-for-help sales representatives and their expectant managers. All I had was a couple of stories to tell them, that I thought might delay the inevitable crash and burn. It was going to be so embarrassing. However after I started telling my first tale, I could see wide eyes, leaning-forward body language and broad managerial smiles that lit the room like bright candles. By the end of my presentation I had in fact told no less than seven stories all woven together. The room was buzzing, my body was experiencing an adrenaline rush and I had finally discovered the explosive quality of the story in presenting.

Since that single occasion, every presentation I do whether short or long will always have a story, and once I start telling relevant stories I absolutely know my presentation will get a big thumbs up.

Left and Right Brain Stories

Most of us know that the left side of the brain is associated with logic and the right side is associated with creativity and the channelling of emotions. There's a great example of an experiment that was carried out at Stanford University some years ago. Students were asked to prepare a one-minute persuasive presentation. The topic each student presented on was to be exactly the same, with half of the class arguing for one point of view and the other half arguing for the opposite point of view. After everyone had given their one-minute presentation, the students were asked to give each other feedback on the effectiveness of their performances, and then asked to write down key points made by each speaker.

Here's the data the Researchers collected subsequently:

- On average, 2.5 statistics were used during the short presentations
- A personal story was used by 1 out of 10 students to make their point
- 63% of the class remembered details from the speeches that used stories
- Only 5% of the class remembered the statistics that were shared

The researchers drew this inference from their research:

"The stars here were the students who made their case by telling stories, or by tapping into emotions, rather than talking numbers or factual data."

So the key to making your audience lean forward and get emotionally connected with you is by using as many stories as appropriate within the timeframe you have. Tapping into their right brain for much longer is a far better strategy that aiming for the left brain. It's not that there should be no left brain information, but keep it to a minimum. Stories help us connect with our audience emotionally.

"People will forget what you said, people will forget what you did, but people will never forget how you made them feel." Maya Angelou.

So let's look at making that emotional connection with the audience. Think of someone you have either seen live or on television that you consider to be an absolutely engaging presenter that uses stories or anecdotes. As you think about this person I'd like you to consider how they looked when they were presenting. Their body language, eye contact and how they moved.

Notice in your mind's eye the smallest details that you may or may not have thought significant and yet these details when you see them again now, make you realise how much they helped that speaker engage the audience.

While that image or movie is now clear in your mind, I'd like you to think about what it was exactly that this excellent presenter said in their stories to really make you connect. How did they say what they said? What was their tone of voice like? And how did they vary their tone as their presentation and stories unfolded?

Finally, as Maya Angelou says:

"People never forget how you made them feel."

So how did this great speaker make you feel as you witnessed their excellent content and message? Run this memory over and over again until you have all the answers you need. It's likely that the speaker stimulated at least three of your five main senses, either consciously or subconsciously. It's likely that they would have used lots of visual references and this could have been done in one of two ways:

- Using pictures, video clips and other visual imagery
- Using words which are visual in their description so that they help stimulate the use of your imagination to create your own visual image in your mind.

There's a high chance that your speaker would have also used lots of words in their stories that enabled you to imagine sounds; either by changing the tone of their voice like an actor or by playing music that created resonance and emotional impact.

Thirdly, the presenter is likely to have stimulated you by your feelings, either using words or pictures deliberately aimed at enhancing and sharpening your emotional receptivity.

Stimulating the audience's visual, auditory and kinaesthetic preferences is one sure way of engaging people when presenting and the more you do it in a presentation the more your audience will remember of the message. Stories don't have to be real to work and they don't have to be yours. They just need to be well told to connect your audience during, as well as after the presentation.

The Three Act Structure of Storytelling

This Three Act storytelling structure is the mainstay of most modern day scriptwriting to tell a story and this comprises of:

1. The Set up
2. The Confrontation
3. The Resolution

Set Up

At this beginning stage of the story it's all about introducing the characters, especially the main hero. This character is usually faced with an incident that in some way means that the protagonist's life will change.

Confrontation

This middle stage is all about the hero having to resolve a challenge that they face by learning new skills required to deal with that specific challenging situation.

Resolution

This is the final act of the story where everything comes together. It's the climax where all the main jig-saw pieces converge and the hero and other characters have a new sense of who they are and their lives as a whole.

This structure has been used for centuries by writers like William Shakespeare, Charles Dickens and Jane Austen, and as long as you have these three main strands to your stories you'll find your audiences leaning forward in awe of what you are sharing with them.

Story Themes

If you think about the types of themes you can have with stories, there are eight that spring to mind which all of us can relate to and you'll find at the heart of most novels, plays, and movies. These themes are:

1. "Slaying the Dragon" – A huge challenge that needs to be overcome.
2. "Renaissance or Renewal" – Rebirth as a result of some new learning.
3. "To Boldly Go where no one has Gone Before" – Going on a journey of unexpected discovery and learning along the way.
4. "The Return Journey" – Going on a journey and coming back feeling refreshed and full of new knowledge.
5. "Rags to Riches" – The journey to success and what lessons you've picked by the experience.
6. "Disaster/Tragedy" – A very sad situation that you can learn many lessons from.
7. "Comedy" – A funny situation that has you in stitches yet that you can learn from.
8. "A Stranger Comes to Town" – A wise person who teaches the town how to be wise also.

There are so many parallels that can be created between these fictional story threads and real life, that we make the link between fact and fiction. Some of the greatest business presenters, such as Steve Jobs, Tom Peters, Les Brown, Anthony Robbins and Jack Canfield are all masters of the art of story telling, using these kind of themes to create an emotional connection with their audiences.

It's also no secret that stories have a profound effect on people's lives and when they are used in presentations they really can help shift a group's perspective. That's why motivational speakers are in such high demand and why a small number can command $150,000 for one two hour presentation.

Using Story Loops

We are looking at *N for Nested Loops* later on. For the moment let's introduce the Loop concept. Some of the greatest speakers ever known use what are known as story loops when sharing their mouth watering tales. On television, any good movie or soap opera will have a number of stories happening at the same time. You recall that the human attention span is about 8 minutes, so the programme director will have a choice. Either tell one story after the other and risk losing the audience through channel hopping, or use story loops. Guess which technique they go for? Therefore in writing a script for a movie there are five story elements.

This is how we would construct the scene breakdown for maximum impact.

We begin the movie with story line number one and then, just as you are about three quarters of the way through this story and at an extremely interesting part of the tale, you then leave that story and move to the second story strand. Soon after, you are introduced to the third story strand and once you get to three quarters of the way through that you might revisit the first strand again but break into the forth story before falling back into story element three before moving on to the fifth. You might then deal with story element five to completion before you complete story four, then story three followed by story two and the end of the movie will finish with the completion of story number one where you first began.

So why do we break off each storyline before we reach the end? Well, it increases the levels of anticipation, curiosity and intrigue. Above all, as human beings we love to have a complete picture in our minds. We crave closure on any story that is started and hate to leave the tale incomplete.

The main difference between a movie and a presentation using story loops is that in a movie you can return to any started story many times, but in a presentation you return to a given story just the once to complete it. Great stand up comedians such as Eddie Izzard, Jo Brand, Billy Connolly and Dawn French all use this technique of story loops to project their unique brand of observational humour to their audiences and very successful as a result.

The best tip for looping stories is to ensure that you create a smooth transition between one story and the next, otherwise people will potentially think you've forgotten to finish off the previous story. The completion of a story loop should be a bonus that comes out of the blue and not expected.

Story Loops in a Nutshell

1. Create a storyboard first for your presentation rather than using slides

2. Make sure you stimulate your audience's visual, auditory and kinaesthetic senses when shaping your stories

3. Tell each story in three parts: Set up, Confrontation and Resolution

4. Use visual images where appropriate, or paint mental pictures

5. Make your story content as emotional as possible to help the audience connect with the right hand side of their brains

6. Use loops to keep your audience on the edge of their seats the whole way through your presentation

Epilogue

An Apprentice complained to his Master Magician:

"You tell us stories but you don't explain what they all mean."

The Magician smiled enigmatically and responded:

"And when you go to buy oranges, do you ask the fruit seller to taste each orange in its entirety for you leaving you with just the skin to take away?"

Chapter 8

Voice and Language

Whether you like or loathe her, a great speaker and presenter of the late 20th Century was undoubtedly the UK Prime Minister Margaret Thatcher. Her premiership lasted just over eleven years from the 4th May 1979 to 28th November 1990. Why was Margaret Thatcher a power presenter? There are several reasons, but one major one is the change in her voice tonality just before she was elected to Number 10 for the first time.

Thatcher's political strategist Gordon Reece happened to meet Sir Laurence Olivier on a train from London to Brighton just before the 1979 election and he asked Sir Laurence for some advice on whether it was possible to change Margaret Thatcher's rather shrill tonality when she was speaking. This led to Sir Laurence recommending the MP to get voice training at the Royal National Theatre in London. Thatcher's biographer later wrote about her training in *Vanity Fair Magazine*.

'Soon the hectoring tones of the London housewife gave way to softer notes and a smoothness that seldom cracked on the floor of the House of Commons…'

Voice tone is extremely important when presenting and in the context of Actor, Broadcaster and Comedian, and is an Actor's master tool. This chapter focuses on two main areas of being a *Power Presenter!* They are *mastery of your voice* as well as *mastery of the Language Patterns* you use. Let's focus on the voice first.

Voice Intonation Patterns

Your tone of voice can have a powerful effect on audiences as long it's done correctly.

Basic voice inflexion patterns can be represented as follows:

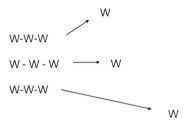

Each W represents a word or phrase in a sentence, and the lines indicate the inflexion pattern rising, level, or falling.

If the line (tone) is horizontal, you are making a statement. If the line (tone) goes up you are asking a question, and if the line (tone) goes down it's a command.

Questions

On the top line in the diagram, if your voice tonality goes up at the end of the words, it will sound like a question. Its tonality subconsciously communicates, *I am asking you a question*. There are some people with regional accents whose tonality goes up at the end of every sentence they speak regardless. It sounds as though they are constantly asking a question and we are not really sure about what they are communicating if we are not from that community.

This is not ideal when presenting, especially if you really want to communicate with confidence to your audience.

Statements

If your voice tonality stays level throughout the whole sentence, then that suggests to the subconscious that you are making a statement. The middle line represents this tonality, which indicates: *Here is a statement and it's on the level.*

Commands

If your voice goes down at the end of a sentence, as per the bottom line of the diagram, your audience will subconsciously take this as a command. Even if you ask someone a question and your voice tone dips at the end of the sentence, the mind will take it as a command. When you want questions, one of the best things to do is to ask a question with a questioning voice tonality whilst raising your eyebrows at the end of the question, and keeping them raised until you get a response.

Raising your eyebrows is a way of signalling to your audience that it's their turn to speak. These voice intonation patterns are what we tend to do naturally, so the more you practise them in the right context with integrity and congruence the more appropriate response you'll elicit from your listener.

What's the Ideal Tone of Voice?

Some may say that there is no such thing as a wrong voice and if we really think about it, any voice is going to be useful in some context.

Many speakers have interesting things to say, it's just that the audience sometimes may not be interested because the audience has the ability to pick up your mental state and add it to the content of your presentation.

This makes your voice tone hugely important in adding credibility and gravitas to what you do on stage. Imagine coming to address three hundred people and speaking with a squeaky voice tonality the whole time. How credible would you be and to what extent would you be able to engage your audience? What follows are some vocal exercises. You can choose one or ideally all of them to practise good tonality. If you're about to skip them and read on, here's something to consider. If you are serious about being world-class or maintaining your existing world-class status, skipping is not an option. How serious are you anyway?

Vocal Exercise 1

This exercise is designed to help you practise changing your voice to match the state you're presenting in and consequently influence your audience into a new state as a result.

Pick a page out of a telephone directory and read the same text for about 30 seconds to a partner while the two of you are sitting back to back. Then have the partner guess which state you are conveying to them.

Two important things affect how you sound. First your state of mind, and second the stance of your body. Changing your physiology will definitely help change your voice and one hormone in our body has a direct effect on how we sound; it's called adrenaline.

Adrenaline stiffens your vocal chords in one three hundredth of a second and this is enough to make a rich and varied voice sound dull and monotone. You'll be pleased to know that the antidote to adrenaline is oxygen and if you breathe really deeply it really does calm you down and allow you to better control and co-ordinate your voice box.

Vocal Exercise 2

This is an excellent exercise to warm up your vocal chords. Stand up straight, bring your shoulders up to your ears whilst breathing in. Now, drop your shoulders whilst breathing out with a sigh, do this 5 times.

Now, push your shoulders straight down whilst breathing in and do this 5 times once more. Now rotate your shoulders backwards 5 times, then forwards 5 times.

Okay stretch and yawn, (It's the only time the throat opens properly) whilst making the sound aaaaaaahhhhhhh...

Now, give your jaw a massage just in front of the ears and act like you're chewing gum with an open mouth. Drop your head down to stretch the neck, then back to the centre and do this 5 times. Move the head to the left and back to the centre five times, and then move the head to the right and back to the centre five times again before over the shoulder left and right 5 times.

Next, pummel your chest like Tarzan and make aaaaahhhhhhhhhh sounds so that your voice tone goes up and down. Sitting down in chair, sit forward with arms on knees, and count to 5 out loud.

Now, sit back in the chair and count to 5 again. Finally sit with your head facing the floor and count to 5. Notice the difference in outcome which is dependent upon the various positions.

Vocal Exercise 3

As already discussed, change the inflexion of your voice and you change the meaning of your message. Say the following with rising and downward inflexions, with a partner standing back to back:

- All together now
- Relax
- Really
- Sit down
- Close your eyes
- That's right
- Any questions

As you listen to your partner, notice how the inflexion changes the meaning of the word or phrase instantly.

Voice Projection

Your voice goes where your attention is. Therefore it's really important to ensure that your attention is where you want your voice to be.

Vocal Exercise 4: The Voice Push

Work with a partner and practise doing the following with a passage from a magazine/newspaper:

1 - Raise your pitch

2 - Quicken your pace

3 - Be more dramatic

3 Final Voice Tips

Whispering is not good for the voice, it's better to speak with a low voice.

Having a different accent is interesting as long as your audience understand you.

The most important thing is to *Open your Mouth* and *Slow Down when Speaking*.

Word Programming

Did you know that we spend approximately 60% of our day in oral communication where we are conversing, influencing, explaining, justifying, motivating, enquiring or just plain telling. The words we use and the Language Patterns related to those words can have either a positive or negative influence on other people.

Below is an example of how the words we use can have an impact on us at a subconscious level. The task here is for you to rewrite the sentences below using only 4 of the 5 words, and re-arranging the words to make a coherent statement. The answers are listed immediately afterwards so please avoid looking at them.

1. Raisins sun in wearily wrinkle.

2. Him was worried she always.

3. Ancient in tombs equips Egypt.

4. Shoes give replace old the.

5. Be will sweat lonely they.

6. Sky the seamless grey is.

7. Should now withdraw forgetful we.

8. Tired change the policies forgetting.

So here are the **answers** to the questions in the same order:

1. Raisins wrinkle in sun.

2. She was always worried.

3. Ancient tombs in Egypt.

4. Replace the old shoes.

5. They will be lonely.

6. The sky is grey.

7. We should now withdraw.

8. Change the tired policies.

"Would you be surprised to learn that in the time it took for you to complete this exercise you have aged?"

This test has probably also affected the way you behave. Scattered throughout the sentences are key words relating to ageing.

This is a re-creation of an experiment that was carried out by the psychologist John Bargh where he asked volunteers to walk to his office and carry out the "word scramble test."

There was an amazing effect on each of the volunteers as all of the words primed their subconscious minds. After the test it was clear to see that the words had a profound, albeit fleeting effect on each volunteer.

As they left the psychologist's office, each one of them walked significantly slower in leaving the office than they did when they entered it. The words related to ageing had a direct impact on their physiology. What the experiment did was to make the *big computer* in the volunteers' brains, their adaptive subconscious, think about the state of ageing. It didn't inform the rest of their brain about this sudden obsession.

All of this talk about age actually influenced their bodies to respond accordingly because your brain is primed to respond to language inputs at the subconscious level. The words that you choose have a big impact on your state and the state of the people you are interacting with. This is also known as a form of semantic priming. With this in mind, how does this relate to the words we use when we're presenting in front of an audience? There are in fact no bad words when used in context, yet we know that some words are not particularly helpful when communicating. They're called DAD words. Words that can be *Ditched, Avoided or Deleted.*

Some DAD Words

Um, erm	No one likes to hear ums and erms
You know	This is a fill in phrase and is better off deleted
Basically	Another fill in word which is unnecessary
Obviously	According to whom?
But	Everything after but is usually linked to criticism
However	Sometimes described as ' the but that went to university'
To be honest	Suggests that everything before that phrase was dishonest

So we've established that the words we use can have a huge impact on the audience, both positively and negatively at a conscious and subconscious level. Moving on to words that will actually move people to action. This is ideal while you're planning a 'Call to Action Exit'. Read the following statements below and see which of them actually makes you the most determined to take Monday off:

Modal Operators

I wish I could take Monday off

I'd like to take Monday off

I want to do take Monday off

I need to take Monday off

I have to take Monday off

I must take Monday off

I can take Monday off

I will take Monday off

I'm going to take Monday off

I am taking Monday off.

Surely it's "**I am taking** Monday off."

These phrases are known as *Modal Operators* and we all use them. When you're speaking to a group you can use any number of modal operators to the audience to influence them to take action. This means if you've reached the end of your presentation and you're urging your audience to do something, it would be an excellent idea to use as many Modal Operators as possible like the ones listed.

Metaphors

A metaphor is a figure of speech that likens one thing to another where there is no obvious connection, however the unlikely comparison makes the message clearer. So for example, you could call a situation *a sea of grief.* Naturally there is no collection of water that also is a mass of grief, yet the metaphor allows us to better understand the overall communication.

Metaphors are excellent tools in presentations. They work well in written content but are especially powerful in visual form. They enable an audience to consider ideas in a different way. The right metaphor can mean a better perspective that you are able to reach the audience with.

Visual metaphors help an audience activate ideas in two channels of their brain as they mix the visual with the spoken. Because metaphors are creative and thought provoking they stimulate the emotional 'underbelly' of the audience's brains. The more metaphors used the more likely the connection and comprehension.

Another tool you can use to connect with is the Great Questions.

Great Questions

3 Golden Rules

1 - Ask questions the audience is probably already thinking about

2 - Use Embedded Commands as Questions

These are commands within in a sentence disguised as a statement. When you ask a question the tonality at the end of the question goes up. When you give a command the tonality at the end goes down. Say this out loud as a question "Can you come here?" Now say it as a command. Notice the difference?

3 - Ask OPEN questions during your presentation and CLOSED questions at the end.

An Open Questions starts with *Why? Who? What? When? Where? How? If?*

Closed Questions demand a Yes or No answer like: 'Do you want to buy one?'

World-class presenters throughout time use the techniques in this chapter. Listen to the *"I have a dream"* speech by Martin Luther King and you will notice all of them being used.

Chapter 9

Understanding Audiences

Imagine the scene. It was just after lunchtime at a Lancashire hotel in autumn and one of those rare occasions when the sun was shining in Manchester. The year is 2008 and also imagine you're just about to run an extremely lively three hour session to a group of experienced sales people and their managers from a large pharmaceutical company.

You've run a similar session for another team from the same company the week before and the audience absolutely loved it, in fact you're sure that managers from the previous week's team must have said something to the managers from the team today because these guys are all smiling and you can sense a feeling of eager anticipation.

Then just before you're about to start, you get some friendly well-meaning, advice from the general manager of the team:

"Listen, I just want you to know I heard how well you went down with the other team last week, but this team is different. They're a bit of an older profile and a lot more experienced so what you did last week probably won't work with them."

Okay he's saying forget what you did and worked so well the last time and do something else.

The question is, what would you do in this situation? Actually you may wish to stand your ground, albeit in a diplomatic way. Understanding audiences is not about arbitrary silos or working groups, it's all about having an understanding of human psychology. We are all human and we all share the same traits. Appreciating what these traits are and how we use them will help you the presenter be more successful each time, together with some additional performance tips. So I did amend some of the stories to fit the older more experienced audience but I stuck with a structure that I knew would work with any audience and got great feedback afterwards from both the people there and that 'helpful' manager.

Content Versus Relationship

If you had to decide between the content of a presentation or the relationship with your audience what do you think is more important?

We normally ask this question during our workshop sessions and it often ends up in a heated debate. Surely it must be the content because that's what the audience is there to hear about. Or is it the relationship, because if you're not particularly engaging then no one will listen to you anyway?

The answer is of course that both are important, but with a twist.

Think of the last time you witnessed someone who really knew the content of their presentation and yet you found it difficult to learn anything from them; in fact you would have learned more if they had just sent you a book in the post. Now, consider someone who you've watched live 'on stage' who before they had even started you knew was going to be a great, and no surprise, it was.

Plus you go away with the message firmly in the forefront of you mind, and like a fantastic movie your brain re-plays clips from it over the next few days. Rapport makes a big difference.

Rapport is the subconscious connection between human beings. Have you ever noticed when people are in solid rapport together they seem to match their body language instinctively? This includes tonality, facial expressions and if you look a little closer they even seem to be breathing in sync!

World-class presenters have an uncanny knack of establishing and maintaining rapport with their audiences, mainly because they spend their time thinking about how they can really engage the audience rather than what the audience thinks about them. They also get themselves into a good state so that their energy will eventually rub off on those present once they have established that rapport. But how does one get into a good positive state?

The Art of Projecting Positive Feelings

There's an old saying: "If you're white hot, your audience will be red hot. If you're just red hot your audience will be hot. If you're just hot your audience will be warm. If you're just warm your audience will be cold. And if you're cold your audience will be asleep".

Just take a moment to think of a time when you've been in the audience and the speaker didn't look or sound particularly inspired by their own subject matter being shared with you.

Replay that memory so you can see the image of that person in front of you while you notice the tone of their voice and how it felt to be in that space and their presence.

Now, think of a time when you've been absolutely captivated by a speaker because they were passionate and excited about their subject matter. Take yourself back to that moment right now. See what you remember and hear again what you heard at the time. Notice how it made you feel and really tune in to this experience, as if you're there once again. Also notice the difference in how you feel compared with when you imagine the uninspiring speaker. So one key to ensuring that your audience is "leaning forward" is to make sure that you are feeling inspired and in a good positive state. Here then is an excellent exercise that will help you achieve this state in any situation.

Turning Up the Temperature on Good Feelings

1. Close your eyes and think of one of the most amazing feelings you've ever had.
2. Replay in your mind what you saw, hear again what you heard the first time and re-engage your brain with that amazing feeling.
3. As you do this, notice where the wonderfully amazing feeling starts in your body and where it moves to. Pay close attention to the direction that it's moving in and where it goes once you stop thinking about it.
4. Now go back to that amazing feeling and let it move again but this time instead of letting it go away, think about it more and more and pull the feeling out of your body and back to it's original source so that it's moving in a circle.

Okay, spin this feeling faster and faster so the feeling starts to spread to every part of your body.

5. Notice that the faster you spin this feeling and the more you spread it throughout your body, the stronger the feeling becomes.

Just imagine going to speak to an audience when you're feeling the way you do now and it's certain they'll all be leaning forward and asking for some of what you've just had. Feeling great about yourself and your presentation is one perfect way of ensuring that your audience feels good too - as long as you match them first and then take them to your higher positive state. This is known as *Pacing and Leading*.

Rapport is such an important subject that we will be returning to it again presently.

The Map is not the Territory

For every audience and every individual in an audience there will be a different take on your message. No two people are likely to get the communication in exactly the same way. *The Map is not the Territory* is an unusual phrase. When you think of it, what springs to mind?

So think about your home town right now. If you wanted to find a road in that town you could use a satnav, or even a map. And you will fully appreciate that the picture you see of the road on the satnav or in the map is not actually the real road, right? It's a representation of the road because the map you're looking at is not the actual terrain or territory itself, hence this phrase.

This concept is attributed to Alfred Korzybski, who in 1931 presented a paper at a meeting of the American Association for the Advancement of Science. The phrase is one of the key fundamental principles of NLP. What we see, hear, feel, touch, and taste in the world is a representation of how we have experienced the world in our brains rather than world itself. This is important, not just when presenting, but in life in general because this means that every single human being has their own 'map' based on their very own mental representation of that world. And this is where it becomes really exciting.

Even if two people are sitting in exactly the same location and experiencing the very same stimulus they will still have two unique experiences because of the three different 'map making processes' that we have already covered in Chapter 5 called *Distortion, Deletion and Generalisation.* If you need to go back and re-read this section to remind yourself, do so now before reading the rest of this chapter.

So our maps are developed in part by these three processes. What you experience compared with reality could be two completely different perceptions and it's why two people with two completely different maps may not be willing to explore the map the other is holding. It often means years of conflict in families and countries. The key is to keep your map updated just like we have to do with our satnavs otherwise you could end up completely lost without knowing it.

Let's think now about how all this relates to the people in an audience and what you the presenter should be aware of in order to deal with mental chatter in your mind as well in the minds of those in front you.

Empowering Beliefs of World-Class Presenters

So everyone has his or her own unique map of the world. In order to have rapport with your audience, it's essential to respect their map of the world first. And bear in mind:

- The success of your message is the response you get back

- There is no failure in making a presentation only feedback

- Resistant Audiences is purely a Sign of *Lack of Rapport*

- There are no resistant audiences, only inflexible presenters

Let's summarise:

Everyone's Unique View of the World

This is because we tend to experience the world we live in according to the three map making processes. As a presenter you should take everyone's view into consideration rather than just your own and then this will help you and those listening to you to look at your content from different perspectives.

Rapport with Others, means Respecting their Map

To have rapport with another person and communicate effectively with them, you need to respect their 'map of the world', no matter how different it is from your own. And whether you approve of it or not. How would you approach your presentations differently if you believed this absolutely? When you're presenting to a group, all of whom have different models of the world at variance with yours, it really can help you if you make sure they know you fully respect their views from the outset.

The Success of your Message is the Response you Get back

Ever been in a foreign country or tried to engage in conversation with someone who doesn't speak your language? Did you even find your voice getting louder? It's funny why people think that raising the voice makes a difference. Most people assume that they control the meaning of what they are communicating. The only absolute way of knowing what the other person thinks of your message is checking out their response.

When presenting, ask yourself:

What meaning did the other person get?

If it is not what you intended, then it's up to you to be flexible and find alternative ways of getting the message across, until they get the meaning intended.

There is No Failure in making a Presentation only Feedback

Learn from every experience for future development, no matter how hard. Every aeroplane has a black box to find out what happened in the event of a crash. It's why aviation is by far the safest way to travel. If you adopted this principle when you presented imagine what it would do for you going forward to world-class status.

Resistant Audiences is purely a Sign of *Lack of Rapport*

When carrying out a product presentation, sales people will often convince themselves that the customer is resisting the product rather than thinking about another way of presenting the offering to lower the resistance barriers.

There are no Resistant Audiences, only Inflexible Presenters

This is built on the last belief, underlining the importance of having behavioural flexibility with your audience. Additionally, if we can communicate with a customer in their preferred learning style, (visual, auditory, kinaesthetic) then they are far less likely to come across as resistant.

So which parts of the A-F Presenting Model are critical in helping us to establish and maintain rapport?

A – Agitate

Because it makes people reflect on their own map of the world from the start and our job is to help them to expand upon their existing map.

B – Benefits

Because if the audience is able to understand why they are there, what's in it for them, and what the positive consequences might be, then you'll find them leaning forward very early on. Let's expand on this with additional tools and insights.

Chapter 10

The G-Z Toolkit

Oh dear. Here's some bad news about being a *world-class* presenter. Once you've mastered A-F and become familiar and confident with G-Z you will then have absolutely no excuse when asked to get on to your feet and present to a group of people!

On a *Power Presenter!* workshop we ensure every attendee understands the G-Z toolkit and gets an opportunity to practise, although the tools are introduced randomly and not in order, as sequenced here. First let's identify what the G-Z letters stand for. Some of these tools we have already covered, but for completeness we have all of them listed.

G for Gestures

Many speakers fail to gesture and sometimes it would be inappropriate or even amusing if gestures came into play, so timing and appropriateness should be a consideration. Also, gestures should never be overdone. By all means act something out using your arms, head, legs and body, but these are not in the same genre as *gestures*.

Gestures are primarily the use of your hands to express a point more concisely though they should never be used just for the sake of it. If you were gesturing every word you uttered it would come across a bit like word signing for the deaf and look ridiculous - unless of course your audience was deaf, but then they would still find it confusing. There are some presentation skills courses that advocate you place both arms by your sides when you present so there are no gestures whatsoever. This is not recommended at all and would perhaps make you look as if you had taken on the guise of a penguin.

A good rule for gesturing as mentioned before is *less is more.* And where possible, limit gestures to the times when you do need to stress your point. Also, operate that 'neutral position' for your hands so that when you are not making a gesture, there's a place for your hands to rest and not look out of place.

H for Humour

Covered already and a reminder here that humour is a tool that's highly recommended when appropriate, although not one hundred percent essential. There will be times when humour is totally inappropriate, yet such occasions are few. Even at funerals, happy memories that makes people smile in an affectionate way makes the message more memorable and powerful.

Humour may be added to any speech, like salt is added to food, by recounting amusing events, acting out something funny that happened to you, considering self-humour, adding appropriate funny quotes and making light of things that happen live at the time of delivery. You don't need to be a professional stand up comedian to be a world class presenter, simply someone who is humour-aware and ready to grasp any opportunity to lift your message with a layer of levity.

I for Invisibility

News readers are masters of invisibility. If they were more visible you'd be watching them and not listening to the news story. An inexperienced news reader is instantly spotted because their delivery draws more attention to them all of a sudden and they probably totally are unaware of it themselves.

The invisibility tool is one you pull out when you have something important or serious to say and you jump straight into Broadcaster Style. Now all focus is on in the message and not the messenger. This sounds easier than you think and does require some practise to be able to pull it off effectively every time.

J for Jack-Knifing

The excellent tool that takes the audience in one direction then yanks them in a totally different one in a split second. Often used as a humour lever, it invariably creates an unexpected surprise element that audiences adore.

(See more the next chapter on Advanced Skills)

K for KISSing

KISS stands for *Keep in Strategic Sandwich.*

It's a technique to start on an unrelated topic, suddenly go into your message then end on the original topic. This is often used in adverts. Like the one where a couple get into a train to suddenly find themselves on a roller coaster ride by accident, then finish the clip talking about the original premise again. This is not a loop however because you come back to the start point really quickly as well as the audience knowing immediately that you've gone off on a tangent.

Another TV advert example is the two guys having coffee when a singer comes in dressed in an evening suit to deliver a message about a car insurance website. If it was just the guys alone chatting in a cafe, viewers would start channel hopping. This keeps the attention going. The sandwich part is the two guys in a cafe at the start and end of the advert which is on both sides of the strategic message part in the middle. This makes it easier to 'consume' what's being messaged too. In a presentation this can be as creative as you dare. Remember that the sandwich are 'bookends' for the real message making it more attractive overall for consumption.

L for Language Power

The ability to be able to get attention from the practised used of key influencing words and phrases that often pack a huge punch. The great news is that you can use the Language Power by simply rehearsing no more than 6 great phrases and then deploying them as needed in each presentation.

(See more the next chapter on Advanced Skills)

M for Magic Bullet

Magic bullets are a prepared sequence or set of words that can be used at any time that's appropriate to create a specific pre-desired effect.

(See more the next chapter on Advanced Skills)

N for Nested Loops

A loop as you now know full well, is where you start a story, break away from it, then come back later on to conclude it. It's the basis of all good drama, be it a play or movie, and of course features in every great novel.

Nested Loops are a collection of stories that are all started and concluded in a *specific order.* The reason a loop works is because it creates interest, intrigue and human curiosity. When loops are done well, the audience is not consciously aware that the story is not yet finished, and when it 's returned to there is always a feeling of completeness and satisfaction form the audience that at the same time underlines the message of the story in a more powerful way.

The 'Nested' part comes when you have say - three to seven stories - that you will start and not complete in a longer presentation and then once all have been started, you will close them one at a time with the last nested loop closed first and in order until the first nested loop is closed last of all. This may sound complex yet if you started with just two stories and worked up to more, you will get the hang of it.

Our advice is to stick with no more than three nested loops regardless of how long your presentation is. In pulling just three off well, the audience are likely to give you high respect.

O for Opening Minds

The biggest requirement for any presenter is to open the collective mind of the audience. If there is no mind opening, what is the point of the presentation? It would mean that your message is already known and there is nothing new for the audience to learn. There are a number of ways to open minds and in the A-F Presenting Model it's at *C for Connect* that you may need to use some additional mind opening tools to ensure it's safe to move to deliver your message.

(See more the next chapter on Advanced Skills)

P for Preparation

Sounds obvious yet you will be astounded how often presentations come to a complete halt through lack of preparation. Here is a list of common challenges that happen when preparation is forgotten or simply not considered.

- the room is too small
- electrical issues
- technology matching issues
- laptop stops working and there's no Plan B
- presentation slides have mistakes
- the missing items (workbooks, pens, feedback forms etc.)
- the need for a microphone
- inadequate signage for delegates
- layout for room not communicated to hotel/location
- poor screen for presentation
- journey time to location longer than imagined creating panic on arrival
- no checklist for any of the above

As the last bullet suggests, **having a checklist** makes all the difference. What follows is a small checklist purely as an example. You should use it as a basis for your own requirements. Having a brainstorm session to think of everything possible before, during and after the presentation would be a great time investment.

Checklist Example - Planning for Success

Before Arrival at the Presentation

✓ Contact client or hotel contact for the event with your environmental requirements, like agreed break times.

✓ Create an introductory message for someone to send out about what you're going to present

✓ Meet with key sponsors of the event (or by phone) to align desired objectives

✓ Direct people to a website before attending, if appropriate

✓ Share feedback from previous presentations

✓ Identify key influencers and start working with them

Preparation for During the Presentation

✓ Ensure room layout is the best configuration

✓ Marker pens

✓ Business cards

✓ Flip chart/pens

✓ Note pads/paper

✓ Mind Map for presenter to refer to?

✓ Visible clock for presenter only

✓ Remote controller

✓ Workbooks

✓ Sound and lighting

✓ Room cleanliness

Post the Presentation

✓ Delegates to leave with branded items like toys, memory sticks etc.?

✓ Suggestions for follow up

✓ Feedback to client/sponsor within 3 working days

✓ Follow up email to managers if needed

✓ E-mail addresses captured

✓ Offer post presentation support/contact to sponsors

Presenter's Bag

✓ Music device

✓ External speaker

✓ Toys?

✓ Flip chart pens

✓ Business cards

✓ Flight case with spare items

✓ Spare laptop or iPad back up

✓ Spare Flip Chart paper

✓ Blu-tac sticky

✓ Delegate paper/pens

✓ Feedback forms/or link info

✓ Master checklist!

Q for Question Skills

Ask great questions and you do several tools all at the same time. You can open minds, create rapport, connect with the audience, stimulate interest and intrigue and take control of your audience in order to impart a message that's taken on board with minimum fuss and effort.

(See more the next chapter on Advanced Skills)

R for Rapport

We all know how important rapport is, but how do you do this with ease and professionalism so that the audience are unaware that you are using the technique on them? Here's the definition:

"A close and harmonious relationship in which the people or groups concerned understand each other's feelings or ideas and communicate well..."

(See more the next chapter on Advanced Skills)

S for Stories

The story is the most common vehicle for travel in any kind of message journey. It can be really short, like a 30 second advert or a novel like *War and Peace*. But a presentation devoid of a story is a complete turn off for an audience. If we go back to the advert. Think of the old fashioned adverts without a story that simply had singing and dancing and a message pushed in your face compared with the story led adverts that emerged in the late 1960s. Indeed some products decided to create a mini soap within their advertising campaign where the stars remained within the project for decades. A great UK example for this is the OXO ads.

T for Tonality

In a song, how important is tone? Silly question. It's everything of course. In a presentation it's equally important. Think of some really awful presentations you've attended and consider what they sounded like. You can probably hear them in your head as monotone (akin to monotonous) and certainly little or no voice variance. Also, when imparting a story, being able to captivate the listener in terms of an emotional is based on your mastery of tonality. And it's a relatively simple business. Just get into the habit of your tone matching what you are saying rather than what most impotent presenters do, which is allow their tone to mis-match their message. Tone, broadly speaking, can be split into soft tones, such as whispers, quietly spoken words, softly articulated sentences, (which is why having a microphone is always better then not having one) then moving into low, medium and high conversational tones to finally articulated, pronounced and quite loud hard tones. The best examples of great tonality are audio books. If the reader of the book were to lack tonality, the listener would probably switch off rather quickly. Always match your tone to your desired message outcome.

U for Understand Audience

There are three audience types.

Sages, Sponges & Self Talkers

In *Power Presenter!* we talk about three other ways of profiling an audience.

- Sages tend to think 'I already know about this' about most topics
- Sponges tend to lap it all up with completely open minds.
- Self-Talkers are having a conversation about your material in their heads throughout.

Needless to say there will be combinations of these groups too. By being aware that these audience types exist, the two groups you need some prepared ammunition for are the *sages* and *self talkers.*

Dealing With Sages

To ensure you quieten the Sages in the room, make statements like:

"I know most of you will probably be already aware of this..."

When you are introducing anything brand new or slightly challenging. If you take the high ground as an 'expert' then they will want to take the higher ground as a Sage.

It's about being a little empathetic. These guys love to criticise so massage their egos a bit.

Dealing With Self-talkers

With the Self-talkers a little more effort is involved. You can spot a self-taker a mile off by the expression on their face. It's quizzical, perplexed or mis-matched with your positivity. To deal with these people stop and ask them a question. Get some of their thinking out in the open rather than allowing them to have their own separate mental presentation going on alongside yours. In short tease out their 'interference' by asking them questions one to one if it's possible and answering the question posed. But be careful. Like Sages they also have easily bruised egos.

V for Visuality

Visuality is about what the audience witnesses as you present. It's not a slide but usually more about the presenter and is the opposite concept to *invisibility.* In the 3 Power Presenter Styles, visuality is about *Acting.*

(See more the next chapter on Advanced Skills)

W for What if?

Though we have Q for Question Skills this question needs separating because it's a potent tool all on it's own. It's the *What if ?*or *Just supposing?* question. The question can be used anywhere in the presentation although there are some obvious places for it.

Introduction

Using the 'What if' question during A for Agitate or B for Benefits works exceptionally well because of the interest and curiosity it instantly generates. It's quite acceptable for example to start with an outrageous *What if?* in order to agitate as well as hint at potential benefits all at the same time.

During the Presentation

If you want to lift the audience that may be flagging which is not a good place to be, or you simply want to take them to a higher plain, then drop in a *What if?* Or, maybe a few of them in succession. This could be staged dramatically as you suddenly stop, look at the audience, make some eye contact, and when you can hear a pin drop - deploy the What if? question.

Exiting

In using one of the 5 exits, the *What if?* option is useful yet again. One of the best exits for it would be the 'Call to Action', however you could also adapt it in the 3 Ender Close asking three *what if?* questions with the most dynamic one being at the end.

X for X-Factor

In the UK television show of the same name, judges are looking for that indefinable quality that makes a particular contestant 'hot property'. In a presentation, using the X-Factor is something well prepared. It will get instant attention and be quite *extraordinary* in nature. In short, jaw dropping.

One example is getting a watch from the audience, having someone smash it into bits and then for the 'magic trick' to be declared as a failure. Naturally there's total silence in the room before the audience are told that it's simply a stunt. Done well, it's fantastic for creating agitation and is an emotional roller coaster ride that can only be described as X-factor material. With the X-Factor tool, the sky's the limit and the only shackles are creativity, imagination and personal paradigms.

Y for Yes Techniques

In influencing an audience getting them to say or even think 'Yes' at appropriate times will be very useful. In order to make this happen, you simply need to be able to use good 'Yes' tools.

Yes Tags

We presume you would like to know how to get a Yes every time, wouldn't you?

Hang on. That was a Yes tool wasn't it? And that was another! To create a Yes Tag use these types of question structures:

- you would, wouldn't you?
- you are aren't you?
- you will, won't you?
- you should, shouldn't you?

Yes Journeys

The Yes Journey is where you tell a story and lead the listener to the thought *'yes'*. It might be wanting the audience to donate some money to a charity on the way out for example. So you tell a story where you get the audience nodding to the emotive appeal of your words, and finally you openly ask a question something like this: "And I saw all these hungry children and thought to myself, would I feel happier and more fulfilled as a fellow human being if by helping them with a single pound coin from my wallet?". (Pause). They are probably thinking... *Yes*. Then you confirm it: "And of course I answered... (Pause)... Yes".

Z for Zenith Points

Zenith means the highest point. On a mountain it's the peak. The reason this is a tool is because presenters forget that you should have mini peak points throughout the presentation and not just at the summit of the message. Zenith Points also happen *really fast*. When planning a presentation, look for places you can potentially insert a Zenith Point which requires some imagination. There was a presentation in the 80s mentioning the prime minister when suddenly a Margaret Thatcher look-alike appeared! What a great Zenith Point.

There could be one in the introduction and maybe a couple during the delivery of the message…so long as the audience are taken to a point which creates an instant high. Maybe you make mention of 'a straight jacket situation', which sounds like a metaphor, but then produce a real straight jacket and ask for a member of the audience's help! This is a classic Zenith Point. You have gone from base station to a summit in a couple of seconds.

Summary

Do review the G-Z tools before each presentation and choose at least a couple to incorporate.

Then at the next presentation chose two alternative ones. In other words, get used to using all of them and notice that by getting comfortable with the tools you are also not only feeling world class, but you are *perceived as world class* by an adoring audience.

Chapter 11

Advanced Presenting Skills

The *6 Advanced Presenting Skill Tools* in your G-Z Toolkit, we perceive as the top tools you should consider using first. They are the gold standard for true world-class presenters. Skills that either need lots of preparation, loads of practice or preferably both. The good news is that with the exception of *Rapport* you don't have to use all of them in a presentation, but if you supplement your A-F with one or two of the six that remain you will ensure greater success through a more meaningful and professional performance.

6 Advanced Presenting Skill Tools:

- Rapport
- Jack Knifing
- Language Power
- Magic Bullets
- Opening Minds
- Question Skills

As you look at this list the one that might appear a basic skill requirement is Rapport. And although it is fundamental, presenters get caught out because they believe that they know what rapport is and therefore tick it off as having been done, when in reality it's not happened at all. Subsequently and the audience come away giving negative feedback.

Rapport done really well is an advanced skill and does require strategy for a particular audience, lots of preparation and even some practice. We have both been on a myriad of presenter workshops ourselves over the decades and it's amazing how the majority of workshops cover where you stand, how you stand, what you do with your hands and so on, yet hardly ever mention rapport. If there was only one skill you could choose in being a great presenter, we would always recommend it's rapport. With this in place, regardless of what the content is, you will always get applause, adulation and respect. Equally, the most amazing content is often *mentally deleted* by members of the audience who have gone off on their own personal journeys of creative mental discovery.

<u>Rapport Checklist</u>

- eye contact
- empathy and wanting to contribute something to audience
- self deprecation
- adding appropriate humour
- genuine humility
- being entertaining
- being challenging in a positive way
- offering a completely new insight on an old idea

Rapport - More Advanced ideas

Building rapport quickly in order to engage an audience is a nifty skill that is different to ways in which one would create rapport when more time is available. It's a bit like having to create rapport with a customer in a shop to make a sale. You have approximately 2.2 seconds to carry this out. What can you do in that smidgeon of time? the answer is: a great deal!

The number one rapport tool is not about smiling, being nice, acting friendly or behaving positively. None of these things equate to what rapport is really about. For example, you walk into a clothes shop and the greeter at the door gives you a big cheesy grin. You immediately feel uncomfortable because you're visiting the store in order to buy a black tie for a funeral. Being smiley has a negative effect here and it therefore can't be considered as rapport.

The number one rapport tool is in fact *Match Plus One*. This is not simply matching because matching a person with a long face won't necessarily create rapport. They can't see themselves and therefore think you are the one being negative. This is where 'Match Plus One' comes into play.
You match what you see but do it *One Step* more positively to get the person to follow you in your direction. Where someone is in a highly positive happy state there's less to do on the 'plus one' side and matching alone will be sufficient.

Now let's place you in front of a large audience. How are you going to use 'Match Plus One?' The solution is to use the tool with 3-6 people individually in the first few moments, also decide where the audience as a whole is.

Maybe you are the second speaker and the first speaker brightened them all up considerably before you came on. This means you do need to start with a similar up beat demeanour to keep the room at the same 'temperature', or it would mean starting all over again. Fast Rapport tools include humour. The only downside is if the joke flops.

One suggestion is to go for your joke anyway and if it fails... pause, look around and say something like this quite seriously:
"By the way that was my one and only joke."
This should get smiles if not a ripple of laughter. If they still remain unmoved you will need more tools!

Further techniques include the 'Hands Up' tool. Ask an obvious 'yes' question, and raise your own hand first so that the audience can match you with theirs. The questions should be empathy based putting yourself on the side of the audience. If they see you on their side, strong rapport will be created quickly.

Ask questions of audience members where you can respond with nods of approval
If you know any names of people answering, using their names in your response to build the rapport with them and a feeling of wanting to connect in general.

Jack-Knifing

A lorry with a trailer in tow is racing down an icy motorway. There's a skid and the front of the transport system meets the back of it in a couple of seconds.

A jack-knife is in progress. It's a fast manoeuvre where two opposites face each other totally unexpectedly. Jack-knifing is used both in comedy as well as straight forward conversation in order to create surprise or make a point. Let's use another Tommy Cooper example who loved jack-knifing in his acts. For example: "I went to see my doctor. (Pause) I had to. He was ill". Here we expect Tommy as the patient, then realise it's the doctor who's unwell. The audience laugh because they've gone down one alley only to end up in a completely different place altogether. The importance of jack-knifing relates to making comedy an easier enterprise for any presenter. Speaker Sir Ken Robinson effectively uses jack-knifing to create humour and therefore rapport with the audience before delivering his main message. In an early TEDx talk he had the audience in stitches and we recommend you hunt this out on Youtube. Just search *Ken Robinson, TEDx & Education.* It's well worthy looking at if you only manage to see the first ten minutes.

Language Power

There are so many powerful language tools that could be mentioned. In fact, ideally it would merit a separate book on this subject alone. Therefore we're going to offer you 3 great Language Power Tools.

1 - The 6 Magic Words

World-Class speaker Bernie De Souza talks about this a lot to sales audiences and it really does work on all sorts of levels. The words are: *Would it be okay with you...?*

This question almost invariably gets a yes with any reasonable request after it. A more formal set of words will bring a pause for thought and a delay in response. Try it for yourself in any situation where you'd like someone to go with your thinking. Equally try it the more traditional way, and compare the results. Here's an example. You want a decision maker to agree to a trial presentation.

Now you could ask:

"Would you be willing to agree to a trial presentation, maybe in January?"

Or you could say:

"Would it be okay with you to do a trial presentation in January?"

Of the two options, which one is easier to say? Also if you are the decision maker, which one of these two questions gets you thinking 'yes' faster? In a presentation, imagine connecting with the audience by using this specific set of words. Couple it with the 'hands up' technique and you have a powerful tool.

2 - The Power of the Negative Suggestion

The human mind can't easily create the opposite of a given set of words. If you say 'don't drop that' to a toddler they are in fact more likely to drop it because the brain sees dropping first it even though you said *don't*. Take motorway messages like *Don't drive while phoning* or *Don't drink and drive.* Think about it. What pictures and feelings are conjured up? Yes, using your mobile and stopping for a drink! So you can actually use this to your advantage. By saying things like:

"Don't feel you have to take notes" or

"Don't feel embarrassed if you didn't know this"

You actually create the opposite thought in the minds of listeners and therefore you can cleverly say it on purpose because in these two examples *you want the people to take notes* and you'd *like them to feel embarrassed* for some reason. By the way, don't feel you must definitely use this tool in your next presentation.

3 - Semantic Priming

Subconscious Semantic Priming is a way of communicating with the subconscious mind that in turn tends to take in words quite literally. This means you can use one set of words that means one thing to the conscious mind while the subconscious mind is hearing something more literal. An example is

I like you and *You like me...*

When you see these words in italics it's what your subconscious hears. However if you express it this way:

"I (pause) like you (pause) think that people should never drink and drive.

Yet your subconscious also hears: "I like you." You are telling the audience that you like them! Or if you use, "You like me," you are asking the audience to like you. Do use this given example and maybe google other examples, of which there are many.

Magic Bullets

This is such a useful tool and when you think about it, not necessarily advanced in its nature, but using it is an advancement that too few presenters ever consider.

A Magic Bullet is a sequence that can be as short as 20 seconds, or as long as 20 minutes where every part of the content you are completely au fait with. So much so, you can do the piece standing on your head or in your sleep.

This would also include the advantage of being able to deliver it on 'auto pilot', where your mind is perhaps working evaluating the audience and people in the room at the same time. Think about the usefulness of this. It means that you may use a magic bullet again and again where appropriate and also pull it out when you need something that you know will work because it's been tried and tested many times. We always suggest to delegates that you have *emergency magic bullet material* when something goes wrong and you need to keep things going while you find a solution. This could be a puzzle or teaser the delegates can do with each other while you work on your problem. In time you can collect all your magic bullets in a single place. It also means you can come up with a presentation at the drop of a hat, any time, anywhere by placing bullets end to end to form a presentation.

Imagine asking a singer to sing a song. If the singer is a pro and a microphone available, they'll be on their feet without hesitation. Music or no music they will perform because they have done this many times before. The song is their magic bullet. It's staggering when interviewing potential speakers and you ask them to present something their reply is: "I haven't prepared anything." Oops!

The first magic bullets that you may wish to prepare and start practising are:

- an agitation (beginning)
- an EXIT (ending)
- an emergency bullet

Opening Minds

There are four excellent ways to Open the Minds of any audience, and there's a big difference between simply getting attention and opening minds. Getting attention is relatively straight forward. Walk on wearing a gorilla suit or activate an air horn for example and these will get attention, but opening a closed mind is a completely separate skill. Some of the most challenging audiences tend to be 'left brained' (like Sages & Self Takers), professions where logic, analysis and detail are high on mental agendas. Such people are often accountants, scientists, doctors and solicitors. With these individuals, opening minds can be tough. It's like walking through a minefield. Take one wrong step and a landline may go off in your face. A basic starting place to ease these minds open is to naturally create rapport first, then try one of the methods.

- deliver the expected with something unexpected of greater value
- offer a them a massive benefit in return for their attention
- demonstrate something that smashes an accepted paradigm
- offer evidence from a highly respect source that backs your message

Question Skills

The best tool to use for asking questions has to be 4-MAT.

The 4-MAT System

Originating from a study in the 1970s from educationalist Bernice McCarthy, she noticed that when she taught children in school, they had different learning styles. In particular, they learned by asking specific questions, which she segregated into 4 categories:

- Some children wanted the reason or purpose – (Why? questions)

- Others wanted facts or an agenda – (What? questions)

- Other kids were very pragmatic or process orientated – (How? questions)

- The remainder wanted to explore future consequences – (What if? questions)

She realised that it was better to structure teaching so that it answered all 4 learning styles in a particular order: *why? what? how? what if?*

In any presentation you need to ensure that you give the information in a way that's suitable for all 4 Learning Styles in the above order.

1. Start with the Why? questions, because until you give reasons, the why people will find it a challenge to listen to the rest of the information. They also will struggle to be motivated to do the exercises and won't contemplate the *what ifs?* It's as if they are on hold until they have a good reason for engaging. Therefore always deal with the suspected why questions with answers before they are asked.

2. Then give 'What?' information. For some people top line information or a 'roadmap' before engaging is critical.

3. Thirdly, deal with the 'How?'. In workshops this is often an exercise. It might be talking them through how they could implement ideas offered back in their own environment or workplace.

4. Lastly, look at the consequences. What would happen if you did this? What would happen if you didn't?

<u>4-MAT in Presentations</u>

The 4-MAT system works well in both one to one and group presentations.

Deliver your presentation with the following Question Answering Sequence:

"This is why this presentation is relevant and benefit you."

"This is what it can actually do for you. Here are the details."

"This is how it will work and how you can utilise it in your business/life right now to get results."

"And these are the consequences if you do it, and these are the consequences if you don't."

Now you are already starting to move to *C for Connect* and strong rapport with the people you seek to inform and potentially influence.

4-MAT Summary

Remember your audience will be thinking things like:

- Why are we here?

- Why this subject?

- What is the talk about?

- What is my desired outcomes?

- How will I benefit?

- If I listen and take notes will I waste my time?

- What if it does prove useful, what then?

- Just Supposing it's a waste time, what then?

So think ahead and answer these questions before they even think them!

Chapter 12

Successful Business Presentations

Power Presenter! has a whole array of business uses and whether you run your own business or are part of a larger community, there are likely to be many regular opportunities to use your newly acquired knowledge to great effect. Here is a partial list of business applications.

- Interview presentations

- Team meetings

- Conference plenary sessions

- Training sessions

- Workshops

- Seminars

- Main platform keynote addresses

- Sales & Marketing presentations

- Technical presentations

- Motivational sessions

- Product launches

- Coaching sessions

- Board room presentations

- Special events

Developing a Power Presenter Mindset

Imagine that in front of you is an 'alternate you'. A 'doppleganger'. A 'you' that is already a World-Class Power Presenter, having an amazing ability to captivate any audience anywhere. See yourself successfully delivering with all A-F steps, with full confidence effortlessly. Now compare this superstar with yourself in the same way. If there's a small gap in performance or even a wide chasm, it's time to continue your development and that normally begins with mindset. The key is that before you even plan your presentation, you should already 'see' it as a success. This is called *mental rehearsal.* Any good sports psychologist would tell you that top athletes stay at the top because of a combination of both physical, and mental practice. They will tell you that the more you rehearse mentally the easier it is to deal with those pivotal moments in a game when you are under intense pressure and open to failure. As soon as you know you have to deliver a presentation, start mentally rehearsing a successful outcome and notice how much better you'll feel consequently when you finally deliver for real.

Well Formed Outcomes

When planning your amazing power presentation decide on well formed outcomes. In other words, making sure that the crystal clear image of success you form in your head is part of your very being. There are 4 pre-conditions for creating Well Formed Outcomes:

- They must be stated in the positive
- They must be initiated and maintained by the individual
- They must be sensory based
- They must be ecological

Stated in the Positive

Often, when you ask someone what they want they'll tell you what they don't want. For example, they may state: "They don't want to feel nervous before a presentation or they don't want the audience to ask them difficult questions".

Here's the challenge. The brain does not compute or work in the negative as we've already mentioned. Don't think of Father Christmas. Who just popped into your head? Therefore, stating what you want in the positive is so much more useful than the opposite. Instead of saying: "I don't want to feel nervous", why not say, " I'd like to feel totally confident". Or that you'd like the audience to feel one hundred percent in rapport with you from the outset.

Initiated and maintained by you

No question you need to be in control of the presentation. The goal you set needs to be your own goal for your own reasons, even if the content has been given to you. You need to ensure that you have well formed outcomes in place so that you know exactly what must be achieved, allowing you to be able to see this through to it's successful conclusion.

Sensory based

Extremely important when planning what you're going to deliver because planning your outcome in at least three senses is a must to align with those listening who are also using those senses. You need to ensure you know what your ideal outcome looks, feels and sounds like. That's why mental rehearsal is such a great tool to use before hand.

Ecological

This is all about the impact that your presentation's outcome will have on those around you. Some useful questions here to test this are:

- How will this presentation affect your life?
- Family? Friends?
- Business or job?
- What will be different as a result of achieving the ideal outcome?
-

Presentation Outcome Tips

Here are some other tips you need to know under broad area headings, to help give you confidence when planning.

Communication and Engagement

Any communication will be memorable if the audience is emotionally engaged.

Brain Processes

The brain cannot process negatives quickly.

Attention 1

Attention continually seeks a fresh object and is diminished by familiarity, which can lead to indifference.

Attention 2

Attention is attracted by curiosity and sustained by interest & variation.

Beliefs and Conviction 1

To be convincing, first you have to be convinced.

Beliefs and Conviction 2

Doubts are reduced by openness but may be increased by over-stressing.

Beliefs and Conviction 3

People's reactions are influenced by those of their peers.

Chapter 13

NLP Tools for Presenters

When you study *Power Presenter!* tools carefully in this book and by attending a *Power Presenter!* workshop, you will notice the content is packed with many ideas that have originated from NLP. What follows is not for the faint hearted because it does require some extra thought, more consideration and lots of practice. However if you are game to explore these tools we are game to share them with you.

Anchoring

Anchoring is a process of getting in to a resourceful state and can occur in any context but are particularly useful when presenting, for example if you wanted to make sure you are in a peak state for success.

Anchors work in the same way that behaviour modification works when training animals. There needs to be a stimulus and a response. Anchors are constantly influencing our behaviour. Like listening to music which can trigger a response, smelling and tasting certain foods can trigger a response also watching a certain genre of movie has the same effect.

Anchors can be created or triggered by any sensory mode and this means that they are very useful to help you to get into a resourceful state when you need to quickly. They can also positively affect the mental state of your audience. The better the anchor formed, the longer it will last.

1. Select a Resourceful State and Decide which Stimulus to Use

Choose a resourceful state that you are looking to have access to in the future. For example, when presenting it might be that you want to be full of confidence. The next step will be to decide what physical anchor trigger you might like to use and it could be anything, such as squeezing your thumb and index finger together.

2. Elicit the state

So if you want to get into a confident state follow these classic instructions:

Close your eyes and think of a time when you felt really confident. As you do this see what you saw, hear what you heard and feel how you felt when you were really confident. Now really tune into this confident state by making the colours richer, the sounds crisper and the feelings even more intense..."

3. Anchor Your State

Now you've fully re-associated with that experience, squeeze your thumb and finger and anchor that state as you continue to see what you saw, hear what you heard and feel what you felt when you were extremely confident.

4. Break State

Just open your eyes and release your thumb and finger and quickly think about something else for a moment.

5. Future Pace

Now, think of a time in the future when you will need this level of confidence. Maybe it's a presentation you need to do today, tomorrow or in a few weeks. See what you will want to see, hear what you will want to hear and notice how it makes you feel to think about this positive outcome. Now squeeze your thumb and finger together and take all those feelings of confidence that you anchored into this new situation. See what you will want to see, hear what you will want to hear and really intensify those feelings. Make the colours richer and brighter and the sounds crisper and the feelings of confidence wash all over you as you take those feelings into the future and come back to the here and now, feeling full of confidence.

Some Tips on Anchoring

- Make sure the anchor you use is unique so that other states and situations don't compromise the anchor.
- Ensure that the state is as intense as you can possibly imagine when you activate the anchor.
- Make sure any movie you create in your mind is as vivid as possible.
- Keep practising using the anchor because the more you practice using it, the more you stimulate your neurology to make it powerful whenever you want to use it.

Different Types of Anchor when Presenting

You can massively improve the state of an audience by setting up and using different anchors for them. Here are a few examples:

Visual anchors could include, movie clips. Pictures or a variety of visuals can without doubt influence the state of your audience. One of the best examples of using *auditory anchors* is in the 'I have a Dream' speech by Martin Luther King. When you listen to the speech, you can hear how the great civil rights campaigner uses his voice, initially low, with a rhythmic tone to gently ensure all of the audience gets the opportunity to hear, see and feel his map of the world, and to consider changing theirs. As time moves on in the speech he becomes even more rhythmical. The tone, speed and pitch increases to the point where you can hear the audience in a frenzy, wildly cheering and supporting his powerful message.

Spatial Anchors

Whatever activity you are carrying out when you're presenting to the audience from the same 'stage position' your audience will be making a subconscious connection between your chosen stage position and your activity.

So where you position yourself and *what you do* can have a surprising impact on the audience. Many top presenters use a stool on stage when presenting so that when they are either telling stories or inviting questions, they sit on the stool, confidently looking towards the faces. Eventually before the presenter actually starts to tell a story or ask a question, the audience knows that it's a story or question because of the association with the stool.

Another example of spatial anchoring is when one presenter follows another. If you are following a presenter who had excellent rapport with the audience, the rule of thumb is to stand exactly where they stood.

As long as you are also good speaker, this maintains the positive anchor already created between speaker and audience. The converse is true if you're following a poor presenter, so stand in a completely different position, naturally.

Circles of Excellence

This surprising tool can be used in a number of ways to get the presenter in a good place mentally...

1. Choose your Resourceful State

First close your eyes and think of an excellent state that you need when you presenting. Confidence? Strength? Success?

2. Think of a Time...

Think of a time when you've demonstrated those things effortlessly. See what you saw, hear what you heard and notice how it made you feel.

Make the colours richer and brighter, the sounds crisper and the feelings so intense that you can feel them from the top of your head to the tips of your toes.

3. Create Your Hologram

Imagine that in front of you is 'twin self' again, a hologram of yourself standing in a circle and give this circle a colour if it helps. This hologram has all the qualities and feelings that you're experiencing right now. Maybe they look super confident, highly motivated and sound extremely inspired. If it isn't quite how you want it, make the adjustments that make you feel better. Allow your intuition to be your guide.

4. Step into the hologram on the circle

When you're satisfied with the other you, step into that hologram in which it is situated.

5. Associate with that Great State

Take on the new perspectives and behaviours into you so that you can see everything from your own eyes, hear everything through your own ears and feel everything right throughout your body. Repeat steps 2-5 three more times.

Think of the next presentation that you'll be doing and for the next few weeks act as if this new you is truly you.

This is an amazing exercise, which is great to do just before you go on stage, run a training session, team meeting or even a one to one session. Practise this as much as you can and see what a huge difference it makes.

NLP Tools associated with the A-F model

The rest of the NLP techniques described here will be linked to the Power Presenter A-F formula. This will serve two main outcomes. The first is to intellectually underpin the key aspects of the formula. Secondly, it will help you to think of a technique with each of the 6 steps. So here are the techniques:

- Pattern Interrupts

- Analogue Marking

- Extended Quotes

- Spelling out words

- Conversational Postulates

- Ambiguities

Pattern Interrupts

Pattern interrupts are the tools you can use to help your audience move out of any state into a more neutral state. Pattern interrupts work by the premise that you can guide a person to a state of your own choosing much easier from a state of confusion. In essence, a pattern interrupt tends to be used to move someone from an intense negative state into a more relaxed neutral state.

Pattern interrupts are abrupt and are excellent when focusing on the beginning of part of the presentation and that's why *Agitate* is such an appropriate description of this key step in the A-F formula.

So imagine you have a whole group of delegates who've turned up to listen to your presentation. Some of them will be thinking about what they'll be doing after the presentation, some of them will be focusing on some of their own problems and are distracted. Others could be genuinely looking forward to hearing you and hearing what you have to say. If they are all colleagues and don't know you, they'll be likely to be mingling with each other and discussing different aspects of work. It makes total sense therefore to enable everyone in your audience to focus on you and your message with a pattern interrupt. So what type of pattern interrupts do world-class presenters use to move audiences from either a negative to a neutral state or even a negative to a confused state?

You could tell a joke or get the audience to do a ridiculous exercise because laughter is the best way to break state as you're changing people's neurochemistry and physiology. Another pattern interrupt is to actually call someone's name, especially if you've only just met him or her.

They'll find it hard to delete your voice and it's likely that everyone else in the audience will stop what they're doing and look around also.

One pattern interrupt that works really well, no matter how large the audience size, is if you ask the audience to stand up and move to a different chair, again this helps to interrupt their comfort mode pattern, take them to confusion and therefore make it easier for them to change their state.

The visual pattern interrupt that is always popular is the movie clip, as long as it's interesting and creates the state you've planned for the audience. Another pattern interrupt that works really well is music at the beginning of a presentation. Often your audience isn't really expecting it and so it helps to change their state quickly. From a kinaesthetic point of view, having things to touch during the presentation, like toys, always creates a sense of curiosity. Pattern interrupts are also excellent in meetings where the delegates always sit in the same place. If you change the room around either during a break or overnight if the meeting is over a couple of days, you can see the 'wow' on the faces of the returning participants. In the G-Z tools, Humour, Jack-knifing, Magic Bullets and Zenith Points are also great pattern interrupts.

Analogue Marking

Analogue marking relates to the way we embed commands into communication and is something that we all do subconsciously. It is usually done when we change our body language, the speed of our speech as well as the volume of our tone.

An example of analogue marking could be a presenter talking to an audience and saying something like "and this is *very, very important* ladies and gentlemen." At this point the presenter may say *very, very important* a little slower than normal, with a deeper voice and maybe a raise of the eyebrows as they look at their audience. If the presenter does this authentically with congruent words and body language then it's likely the audience will not only take note during the presentation, they may also take notice long after the presentation has finished, purely because this message has gone into the person's subconscious minds.

Extended Quotes

Here you give your message in story form and the punch line may be a quote that someone said in the story. The purpose of this is to help you to connect with the audience in a way that you can build the credibility that you want with your message, no matter how direct it is. Here's an example:

"When I was a manager, I used to have a meeting with my own manager and I always wanted to impress her. I would turn up with all my data, analysis and explanations, plus recommendations to our meetings. She would give me advice and direction and as she told me what I needed to do, I'd say "I know," she'd continue to keep giving me advice and then I'd continue to say "I know".

One day we had a meeting, she was giving me advice and then I said "I know" and she looked me in the eyes and said :

"To know and not to do is not to know. End of of meeting."

What a great quote to use when you're in front of a whole team of managers who feel like they are pretty knowledgeable and where there is danger of them just nodding with compliance and then deciding to take no action afterwards.

Spelling Out Words

This effectively draws your audience's attention to you and the message because you spell out the key message. It also helps your audience to R-E-L-A-X. Great to use at the beginning and the end of the presentation, namely at Agitate and Exit.

Conversational Postulates

These are questions we could answer with a YES or NO but we choose to give a behavioural response instead rather than a literal answer. Have you ever phoned a friend's home and asked their young child something like:

"Hello Johnny, is your Daddy there?"

You're then expecting young Johnny to say:

"I'll just go and get him", and instead Johnny just answers "Yes" and stays on the phone. The question you've just asked is a conversational postulate and Johnny's right to answer with "yes" or "no". However as adults we allow that question to bypass our conscious mind and become a subconscious command. Most adults when asked, "Can you close the door?" don't tend to respond by saying "Yes". These questions are useful when presenting because they help to maintain rapport with your audience and avoid sounding too dictatorial. Some examples of conversational postulates in presenting are:

- Can you picture doing this?

- Can you imagine doing this?

- Would it be great to feel this good?

- Do you know that you know it already?

- Could you open your mind for a moment?

- Can you space yourself out round the room?

(MORE)

- How easily do you think you can do this?

- Does this sound like it will work for you?

- Do you think you can make the changes you want?

- Wouldn't you just like to drift into that peaceful state now?

- Wouldn't you mind writing down a couple more notes here?

Ambiguities

Ambiguities are the meat and drink of most comedians. The English language is so laced with double meaning, it causes you to subconsciously search for the real meaning of what you said when you consciously use vague language. There are different types of ambiguity and they all have great uses when presenting.

Phonological Ambiguity

Words have different meanings and yet they sound the same. It's a form of pun. This language completely distracts the conscious mind and your audience tends to go into a trance as their brain tries to sort out the ambiguity.

English speaking stand up comedians play on this, as do comedy scriptwriters. So here are some examples of words, which can contribute to phonological ambiguity:

- Write/right/rite

- There/Their

- Here/Hear

- Wandering/Wondering

- Buy/by

- In security/Insecurity

An example of how you could use them in everyday presentations:

As you begin to **wander/wonder**, **buy/by** now … (Sales Presentation)

Why don't you all stand up for a **spell?** (Magic Circle Meeting)

How are you going to make the most of your **days/daze?** (Hypnotist Conference)

There's a classic comedy sketch from "The Two Ronnies" called *Four Candles* where one of the comedians goes in to a hardware store and asks for 4 Candles and the storeowner is trying to sell him garden fork handles. It's one of the most popular comedy hits on YouTube and when you see it you'll understand why. Using phonological ambiguities is a great way to use double meaning to inject humour into your presentations, especially if you're speaking to an English speaking audience and English isn't your first language.

Chapter 14

Setting Up a Successful 'Stage'

If you've had to run any kind of presentation before you've probably wondered what might be the best way to set the room up in order for the people get the best from the event. If you've never thought about this before now is the time because the more attention you pay to the delivery environment, the more likely your presentation will tick all the right boxes as your audience enters for the first time.

Room Layouts

Presenters often ask where is the best place to stand. This depends on the size of the audience. If you're speaking to up to forty people the best configuration is a U-shape with chairs and no tables. Tables invariably create a barrier and make rapport much more of an uphill struggle. Some delegates love to use a table as body armour and ensure they are 'safely' tucked away behind it.

With forty to a hundred people a change of strategy is on the cards and this may involve arranging the chairs in three sections. The middle section of chairs faces centre stage straight on, the section opposite stage left is at 45 degrees to the centre and the same configuration opposite stage right.

Both of these layouts will help you to establish and maintain a connection with the people present and allow them to feel your energy and positive vibes. The layout of the delivery space will always have a significant bearing on the outcome.

There are also some layout patterns that tend to make you work twice, if not three times as hard, which you need to avoid. More on this presently. Let's start by looking at the stage area itself which can simply be the front of the room.

The Staging Area

Just like when you go to the theatre, you have a staging area when presenting. The figure below highlights the different parts of this.

Upper Stage Right	Upper Stage Centre	Upper Stage Left
Down Stage Right	Down Stage Centre	Down Stage Left

Audience is here

Notice the descriptions of left, right and centre stage refer to your position, not that of the audience. As you prepare your talk, keep this image of the stage in mind so you may mentally rehearse your presentation. Think about which part of the stage you'll use when you start with *Agitate*, where and how you'll establish *Benefits* with good eye contact and open body language that creates a relationship.

Decide how you will use the stage to *Deliver the Message*, and where you will stand when you deploy analogue marking. Finally where you'll be when you're in *Exit* mode. The ideal situation is that you really maximise the use of the staging area rather than be perched in one position for most of the presenting time.

Room Layouts

Where numbers of delegates and adequate space allow, you should consider using the 'U' shape layout with just chairs if you're running a training event . Note books can go on the chairs. Tables and chairs if it's a more formal meeting. In the event of lack of space or excessive numbers, then theatre-style could work. Let's look at the pros and cons of each of the different room layout configurations.

U-Shape

A series of conference tables set in the shape of the letter U, with chairs around the outside or just the chairs arranged in a U-Shape without the tables.

This style with the tables is often used for board meetings, discussion groups where there is a single speaker, an audio-visual presentation, or other focal point session. Without tables this style works for training events where the speaker is looking to connect with the delegates and where the group members are asked to participate in a practical way. Avoid the "U" shape set-up for groups greater than 40, because the sides of the "U" become too long and you'll have to work really hard to enable all of the delegates to participate at the event.

Positives

• Great interaction space between you and your audience

• Good interaction between participants

• Ideal when movie clips, visuals or speakers are involved

Theatre Style

Seats or chairs in rows facing a stage area, head table for speaker.

This is the most popular set-up when the attendees are there as a conventional audience. However, it is not recommended for food events and make sure there is enough "elbow room" if note taking is required. It's a very flexible room set-up. Rows can be circular, semi-circular, straight, or angled towards the focal point. You can arrange each row so that attendees don't have to look over the person in front of them, although this will increase the space required. If using banquet type chairs, space them 3" to 6" apart, as these chairs are normally narrower than most people's bodies. If you have the space, allow for 24" between rows, to allow attendees easy movement in and out of the row.

Positives

Good for large groups when reading/writing are not required.

Considerations

- You need to raise the height of the stage so that everyone can see the speaker with a large group
- There's no writing surface
- Minimal group interaction unless you have place in front or behind the chairs for practical activities.

Classroom Style

Rows of conference tables with chairs facing the front of a room, providing writing space for each person. This set-up is ideal for taking notes, meetings that need lots of handouts or reference documents or the use of other tools, such as laptops and tablets.

It's the most comfortable set-up for a very long session and allows water or other refreshments to be placed within easy reach of every attendee. If you have tables that extend beyond the stage or podium, then they should be angled towards the speaker. Make sure that you allow for approximately 2" of space per person at each table. If you know that lots of materials will be provided then more space may be required. The minimum space between tables is 3". If the room space allows, provide 3½" for ease of movement in and out of the rows.

Positives

Presenter can see all participants

Accommodates large groups in less space

Considerations

Minimal interaction opportunities

Participants can only see each other's backs

Boardroom Style

A rectangular or oval table set up with chairs around all sides and ends.

This layout is often used for board meetings, (bored meetings?), committee sessions or discussion groups. Many hotels and event venues have rooms with permanent conference tables in a variety of shapes. When these tables are not available, standard conference tables can be placed together to form a square, rectangle or hollow square. Remember the larger the set-up, the harder it is for attendees to see the others at the end opposite to them.

Positives

Great working space for each delegate

Can be a positive cosy working environment

- Not ideal for audio-visual presentations unless you've a TV fitted to the wall at one end of the room
- Not ideal for speakers as their movement tends to be restricted as there's no 'stage area'
- Not good for larger groups

Hollow Design

A square conference table arranged in a square or rectangle, leaving the centre open. Seating is placed around the outside of the tables.

When you have larger meetings of 12 to 30 people in your audience, in which group interaction among attendees is important and meetings when the event does not have a designated leader or presenter. This is a useful room design that provides workspace for each person and good communication and visual lines for each person.

Banquet Rounds Design

This is a group of round tables, normally seating 6-10 people. They are usually set to facilitate serving food, usually in a hexagonal or square design. Half Rounds

is seating around half of the table so all are facing towards the front, allowing everyone to face a presenter.

Banquet-style is the set up plan of choice for most meal functions and wedding receptions. In addition it is also useful for small business meetings and breakout groups involving interaction and/or note taking.

Often people use this for training and conferences, but the challenge with this is that people tend to have a lot more sideways conversations and they can be slightly more raucous than U-shape or theatre style. This is not recommended for learning.

Reception or Cocktail

Here you have small round cocktail tables, usually 15-30" in diameter, with chairs. Normally all tables are positioned uniformly to allow for even coverage of the banquet room and standing room only. This configuration is great for cocktail parties and receptions and not for presentations or training events.

Layout Summary

The best configurations for any event are U-Shape for smaller groups (up to 40 people) and Theatre Style for larger events (over 40 people).

Other Environmental Considerations

Music should be playing in the room prior to the start of your presentation and during breaks, as well as at the end of the day. It goes without saying that the music should be uplifting and motivational. If you're running a workshop or doing a session on stage for longer than a couple of hours, a chair on wheels or a stool is another option to be considered so that you are not standing for an excessive period. Finally, if you imagine the delivery space as being a very special place, then when you first enter it, the feeling should be intrigue bordering on wonder, while the word that should enter you head should be "Wow!"

Chapter 15

Power Presenter Fast Track

A popular question asked time and time again is whether there's a fast track to becoming a world-class presenter and annoyingly the answer is both 'yes' and 'no'. (Sorry!)

Let's start with the 'no' side and get this out of the way quickly. There is nothing we know of that would ever take the place of practice, experience, failing and learning from the mistakes, and being coached over a sustained period to get you to where you want to be. This can be seen with great speakers like Ricky Gervais who gets better as time goes on and even he will probably admit that some of his riskier material doesn't always come off, but he certainly doesn't let that put him off inching forward.

This being said, there is lots to say around the 'yes' response. Firstly, in almost any walk of life there are things you may teach another person that are easy to learn and yet when others see you doing these things you are immediately seen as an expert. One funny example is karate. We were taught board breaking by a karate expert with all the moves and sounds and then we passed this 'black belt' move on to delegates in sessions.

The amount of training time was approximately 11 minutes, then 16 minutes later the delegates who had zero experience in chopping pieces of wood in two with bare hands were doing it.

If you had walked into the room at the point of chopping the wood in two slices you could be forgiven for believing you were watching a black belt in action. Actually, you were. That single move had been coached to black belt standard, albeit one single move, and so the delegate technically was a black belt for that single move even though they knew nothing else about Karate!

The same can work in presenting skills, which is why A, B, C, D and E is so powerful. Prepare your A-E with F for follow up and this alone will distinguish and differentiate you from the 99% of presenters that have no model or structure and are often completely haphazard. So let's say you have an important presentation coming up and one hour to prepare. Now pulling a rabbit out of the hat in this scenario really would be *fast track!* We have to assume you have content to share which you are familiar with but perhaps written as notes. How do we get you ready to knock their socks off with just 60 minutes prep-time?

When we look at these 60 minutes, they don't have to be used from beginning to end without stopping. You can in fact spend the time in chunks too. This means there's never an excuse to saying you simply can't find the time. If you desire real success, there's always time.

Do consider how you may also use the following fast track as a manager or leader. If you like our approach, do pass it on to your team. Where it is unlikely to replace a live workshop, it will certainly get people on the right footing and can even be suggested in the morning when the presentation is due at lunch time or that afternoon.

The first 24 Minutes

Get your scripted material into single words or a short sentences. Imagine you have 6 pages of notes. If they are in a file, separate the content into short paragraphs and give each a name in red (or short sentence).

Let's assume the topic is *'Technology in the next 20 years'*

1 First paragraph is an introduction to your topic (call it **INTRO**)

2 There are three sub paragraphs in the introduction. Firstly a definition to what technology is. Secondly some examples of great technology to date. Thirdly examples of new thinking around future technology (call this **DEFINE, GREAT EGs, FUTURE EGs).**

Now we have the introduction as 4 key words or phrases. Do the same thing with the rest of your script until you have the entire content as key words or reminder phrases.

By the way, if you have so much content that you think it could never be done in 24 minutes, you don't have a presentation, you have a long lecture or mini-workshop and we are not talking about either here. If it is meant to be a presentation and there's too much content and detail, consider major surgery as it will only improve your message. If the content is essential then give hand-outs of your script to those who would value the detail at the end. (F, for Follow up allows you to email the detail to them after the presentation).

The script should also be in the following sections:

1 - The introduction

2 - The benefits to the audience

3 - The main message

4 - The ending

Minutes 25-36

In the next 12 minutes you need to be clear on the following:

a) Do I have a Great Title? If not - get your skates on and think of one. If it's quirky or slightly controversial even better. For example: 'Do we really need anymore technology?' This would create curiosity where 'Technology in the next 20 Years' gives away your 'plot' and who would watch a move where the plot is self evident?

b) What's my Primary Objective? Be clear on what 'success' would look like in this presentation. If you have no idea, then the audience certainly won't be working it out for themselves.

c) What's *Agitate* going to be? Okay, to be fair, this isn't as straight forward as we would like. Often delegates are challenged to come up with a good agitation

Fast track possibilities are:

- A movie clip from YouTube streamed live as your session starter
- A quote from a book or newspaper found on line which is controversial
- Starting with the 'hands up' technique.

Here's how you can use the Hands Up technique. Answer a question that you know most of the audience would agree with. For example, your question is:

"Who here believes technology is only recently getting started here on planet earth and there's lots of exciting new things just around the corner that we will benefit by?"

The chances are most of the room will raise their hands. Then you exclaim:

"I don't agree," Pause. Look around at the faces. It might even have gone very quiet. Hey presto you have successfully started the Presenting Model with *Agitate*.

You simply then pick things up with:

"My concern is that no matter how good technology becomes, it should never remove the basis of being human.

Did you know that 24% of eleven to fifteen year olds in the UK prefer to communicate by social media rather than by face to face or even by telephone?"

There you go, you should really have leaning forward at this point!

One more. Have something bland written on a flip chart. In our example on technology this could be: 'Technology is so cool'. Now walk up to the flip chart and tear off the paper then rip it up and throw the paper over your shoulder. Then go from the Pause in the previous bullet point. Some of you might be thinking, *a bit over the top?* and it might well be for some but we assure you it would certainly get the audience's attention. Often workshop delegates guess that A stands for 'Attention'. Yet you can get attention by simply clearing your throat and then announcing that your presentation is about to start. The question is, will this be enough to sustain their interest and curiosity?

Minutes 37-44

Create 2 Magic Bullets.

<u>FIRST BULLET</u>

Know what your first three sentences are going to be by heart and then practise them.

<u>SECOND BULLET</u>

Now work on your Exit. Chose which of the 5 Exits you will use then plan how it will sound. Once again, practise it. After these 12 minutes you should be super confident with your opening and ultra confident with your Exit.

The Final Minutes

The 16 minutes left takes place at the location. Get there early and rig the room so you don't need to look at your script. There are a few ways of doing this. If you ask for 3 flip charts to be there, then have one up front and the other two at the back of the room in the two corners. (Not needed if you can have an auto cue or visual prompter). Now write up your key words on these flip charts, *but in code!* We appreciate that this sounds odd, but if people walk in and clearly see your prompts then they know what you are up to. If they just see some odd words on a flip chart they are probably thinking it relates to a previous meeting. It is in fact your aide memoir. A second way of doing this is to place key words and phrases on A4 size paper and blu tack them on upper walls and rafters where the audience will not see them easily, but you certainly can from the front. If you do have access to a screen and remote, then type the slides in large print using powerpoint and have the screen facing you. With a remote you can prompt yourself as to what's next on your agenda. If you have been given an auto cue device then restrict its use to prompts and not word for word scripting.

The Last 3 Minutes

There's now 3 minutes of prep time remaining. How best to use this? Stand at the front of the empty room and look into every nook and cranny of the space. Get familiar with it and feel confident in yourself as you do this. Check out your 'script' and run your eyes over the intro and ending again.

Now blast out your three sentence intro one more time. Finally make a mental picture of this same room with people in it. Imagine looking at them and still feeling confident and even passionate about getting your message out. Imagine them responding, liking you, liking what you say and applauding you at the end. Now, you're ready.

Over the years we have seen people read these instructions and think it impossible to follow through. Yet on so many occasions delegates have come back to us with their amazing success stories and some even saying they had a few minutes left over. By the same token, when people have more than 60 minutes they can really go to town on good preparation and really make it count.

Three Bonus fast track ideas

1. Search for that 'killer' video clip. Search for something on YouTube or Vimeo that will stimulate the many 'visuals' that are likely to be in the room. A great clip will always reflect favourably upon you, the person who chose to show something that gave the audience some personal pleasure.

2.Get a couple of famous quotes. Don't over do this, but do hunt for something that someone well known said that would support your overall message.

3. Have something in writing. Whether this is something you handwrite on a white board or flip chart, or a slide that pops up with it on. People are prepared to believe in things more so when written down rather than just spoken.

Chapter 16

Marketing Yourself as a Presenter

Whether you are a coach, trainer, consultant, professional public speaker, corporate manager, stand-up comedian, business leader or television presenter, it could be in your interest to market yourself and get your name in lights. Not every speaker will want to push their name out into cyberspace, and so this all depends on how serious you are to do lots of public speaking, whether within your community, company, business or potentially all over the world. What follows are *7 Top Tips* that could help you in your quest. What's of paramount importance is making a decision that this is what you want to do and the fervent desire to achieve your outcomes. First, an overview of the top tips and then some more detail.

The 7 Top Tips

1 - Decide on your Game

2 - Get a Shop Window

3 - Create a Messaging System

4 - Write a book

5 - Get interviews

6 - Network

7 - Get an Agent

1 - Decide on your Game

Decide on your Game? This simply means: What ball park are you wanting to be in? If you think of any famous presenter you will immediately be able to pigeon hole them. Now although this sounds a bit underwhelming, it's critical if you want to market yourself. At the time of writing we are unaware of a top presenter who is an all rounder and can speak on any topic as a specialist. Just about every successful presenter has a slant. Consider Paul McKenna, Barack Obama, Kelly Hoppen, Tony Robbins and Deborah Meaden. Each individual here can be pigeon holed for their speciality. It's what makes them well known and therefore easier to market. It's like having a product that makes the tea, helps you exercise and cleans your car. How easy do you think it would be to advertise and market this product?

Getting clear on what your slant or area of expertise is a must if you are going to not just get well known, but actually hired on a regular basis. The way to crack this for those of you who don't appear to know what your speciality is would be to do one or all of the following:

- ask other people who know you
- think of a new slant on a standard subject
- consider taking a controversial position on something well known
- do a brainstorm session with people who know you
- look on Youtube for inspiration around your potential subject area
- invent a new concept, product or twist on your subject then write a book

Let's take a fictional Mike Carter who is a business trainer. Mike coaches on no less than 17 topics, including customer care, management principles, time management, sales & marketing and so on.

Then he makes a decision to choose one topic to really concentrate on, Leadership. He thinks of a twist on the subject, which differentiates him, then writes and self publishes a book. Suddenly he stands out. People know what they are getting in inviting him to speak and it makes it easier to make a decision to book him for events. There is the thought that by Mike specialising in leadership he would not get hired on any of the other 16 topics he can speak about, yet this isn't the case at all. He simply leads with Leadership. So a conference on Customer Care could still be on his radar but he approaches organisers based on his Leadership prowess.

2 - Get a Shop Window

One of the top two ways people still buy goods today is from a shop or online. Both of these methods have a place to view products. The former uses a shop window, the latter uses a website or app. This makes it easier to buy something, and the easier it is to buy, the more sales are made as a result. It appears ludicrous when you visit a website for example and want to make a simple purchase that you need to fill in umpteen screens, boxes and seemingly have to input unnecessary information. Similarly, if you go to a speaker's website the following isn't clear then you must suspect this individual is either not professional or simply doesn't know what a poor impression they are giving surfers to their site.

Here are the 4 'Deadly Sins'

- No clear idea on what the speaker's speciality is
- No evidence she/he is credible
- No examples of their work (video clips)
- No idea how to book them (effortlessly)

Some of the reasons presenter websites fail include:

poor images of the speaker, badly shot homemade videos that do the speaker no favours, poorly written text, a cheap looking website, and the number one reason: a website that doesn't immediately grab attention due to a lack of overall design.

Get yourself a biography too in order to send out when requested or to be used to introduce you at an event you are speaking. However have two. A long complete one on your website and to send out to people, but then a shorter punchier one that lasts 30 seconds or less when read out to an audience just before you start your presentation.

Then consider finding yourself a video maker who can create a YouTube channel for you. In getting your own channel remember it's not a one off event. You need videos regularly posted, which also applies to your website, although you can of course connect the two. Finally there's a big difference between having your speaker pictures taken by a friend and having them taken by a professional photographer.

The latter will mean a small investment but can make a big difference when it's to be evaluated by decision makers. It's all about quality photos that give the eye of the beholder confidence that you can deliver on your promises.

3 - Create a Messaging System

Programs like *Mail Chimp* help many speakers keep in touch with their potential prospects, but also with friends and contacts who may know someone. It's so easy to be forgotten by 'hiding' yourself from the world and then simply getting overlooked. The idea is to send a blog post or update about yourself regularly, which is usually a helpful tip of something the recipient would value personally rather than it be an advert about yourself. The frequency is also important.

It's suggested as once a month. Sending weekly messages is costly from a time point of view and can put you under lots of pressure, yet the receiver's reaction to seeing you pop up in their in box every week is more the point. People can become tired of seeing you so often and then invariably start looking for the unsubscribe button. Probably the best way forward to messaging and reminding people is as follows:

1 - Decide on a format to use like *Mail Chimp*

2 - Create a 'shopping list' of potential topics, ideas and tips you can send out

3 - Remember the content must match your speciality

4 - Always include a visual or video clip

5 - Any video must be easy to play instantly

6 - Label the post by the month like 'January's Update'

7 - Ensure it goes out on the same day every month

The best content would be things that would get *your* attention. This means stuff about your last gig and where you are speaking next month is probably going to turn a lot of people off. However finding a YouTube clip that's short and fun to watch with a speaker message attached would probably go down well and link you in a positive way.

4 - Write a book

Today it has never been easier to get into print. Self publishing can be done with as few as a dozen copies to start and there's no excuse not to have a book published. One thing to decide upon immediately is whether you do in fact want to self publish or be published. Self publishing is quicker and will give you all the proceeds from sales, where a publisher will charge you to buy copies of your own book and a small percentage on sales.There are publishers looking for good business book titles but don't expect an up front fee unless you are already in print and successful. Think about being in front of a distinguished audience and introduced as an author. Being a published author gives you credibility and a point of instant reference as people are still impressed if you can claim a book under your belt on your chosen subject.

What a great way too to get a booking. What better business card to a decision maker than your book in their hands with your autograph in the inside cover. It also makes it a great way to send people away after your presentation with your book in their hands.

The biggest block perhaps is thinking you can't write a book. Websites like elance.com allow you to find a ghost writer for a lot less than you may imagine. And if it's not the writing part that stops you, and it's more about time, then consider writing a chapter a week of about 3,000 words and 12 weeks later having a first draft! A graphic designer could be found to do the cover on sites like fiverr.com and within no time you have your book that simply needs a proof read and perhaps an index; things that can also be farmed out.

Assuming your problem is the mistaken belief that you have no time to write, start by thinking up a great title which by the way also needs a bi-line. So *Power Presenter!* is the title of this book and the bi-line is: *The Fast track to World Class Presenting*. Without the bi-line under the title you are missing out on an additional lever to help sell your work. This doesn't apply to novels as a rule, but certainly does apply to movies today. A movie without a bi-line means the title is so strong that it doesn't need one which is rare these days.

5 - Get interviews

When you see people being interviewed on television or in a journal or magazine, eighty percent of the time they have gone out of their way to arrange it. Being interviewed is any speaker's holy grail when it comes to good publicity. A way to do this would be to approach a newspaper or on-line periodical and offer yourself as a potential interviewee. This would also apply to television and the radio. Here having a great shop window and good book under your wing will help enormously. Very often you make it easy for the organisation or person you are approaching by even offering them the questions to ask, which they will gratefully grab to make their life easier.

You may also consider getting your own interviewer, making a video clip and sending it by e-mail as a suggestion or indeed the finished article. If it's well crafted and has good content it would be tough to say 'no', provided you have sent it to an appropriate publication. Do remember that an interview can also be forwarded as a script, and if it's not an interview, a well written article may also be a good route.

6 - Network

There is a phenomena that started off in the late 80s that's still very much in evidence today, which is the *Business Breakfast Club*.

Here people meet each month to handshake and network live in a way that doesn't happen when you send a one sided message by e-mail.

The three dimensional aspect of a live interaction offers a more significant connection and as a result increases the likelihood of being spotted for an upcoming event. This is especially the case when you are also prepared to help the other party.

Networking can also be handled in a more proactive way. Consider offering a 'trailer' presentation to companies and organisations who would potentially have a need for guest presenters and speakers. This isn't a freebie, and is most certainly a trailer or small glimpse of what may be expected from you. Trailers should be no longer than 10 minutes, although there is one big proviso. Whatever you do in 10 minutes it has to be good! In fact we would go as far to say, jaw dropping. It must also be a teaser where the audience want more but can only get the rest if they book you. One approach is using a number between 3 and 7.

For example, if you are offering the "The 6 Leadership Insights for the Next Decade" and offer one of the best ones in your trailer, naturally the audience are now intrigued and want to know what the other five are. When using the trailer method, simply ensure you offer your very best content like they do in movies. Although it has to be said that sometimes all the best bits are in the trailer of a new movie, which can be a disappointment when you go to see the full movie and realise the fact.

7 - Get an Agent

The last suggestion is to get an agent. This is a tricky one because if you don't have an inside track on how agents work then you can get the wrong idea. Most agents do very little marketing on your behalf, they simply field enquiries and may decide to call you as a result. Bear in mind they have others on their books which is why having a strong differentiation is so important. It's also true that agents will have favourites. If they put up a speaker to an event and get poor feedback they are likely to avoid booking that speaker ever again. On the other hand, if your agent uses you regularly and always gets a big thumbs up, he or she is more likely to keep their own income stream flowing by going with you more often. The question is how do you get an agent who will view you in this way? Where do you start?

In looking at all the previous ideas here, and by acting on most or all of them, you will be better placed to search for an agent. Sending them some clips and a biography is usually not enough, even if these items do bring back a positive reply. Being on an agent's books means nothing. Being busy on an agent's books is another matter entirely.

The way to do this then is to sell yourself to the agent. Put them on your Monthly Messaging System, and invite them to an event that would impress them. Always get every presentation videoed and send your agent a clip as soon after the event as you can. Then there's the ultimate idea!

Get yourself a presentation at an event and ask your agent to deal with it. In other words, give away a percentage of the fee on purpose to get the agent's attention. This is also an opportunity for them to see you present as they are getting a fee to attend.

If you want an agent, and having one is certainly a good idea, do make sure you sell yourself to them so they see you as a safe bet who will make them money. After a while you will then notice regular work from them, meaning you have cracked it.

Final Note

If you have been inspired to become a better presenter, check out otd.uk.com and consider joining us on a live workshop. You may also contact us with any questions. Here's us wishing you every future success as a ***world-class power presenter.***